EMPTY

OUT

THE

NEGATIVE

Make Room for More Joy, Greater Confidence,
and New Levels of Influence

JOEL OSTEEN

New York • Nashville

ALSO BY JOEL OSTEEN

ALL THINGS ARE WORKING
FOR YOUR GOOD

*Daily Readings from All Things Are
Working for Your Good*

BLESSED IN THE DARKNESS

Blessed in the Darkness Journal

Blessed in the Darkness Study Guide

BREAK OUT!

Break Out! Journal

Daily Readings from Break Out!

EVERY DAY A FRIDAY

Every Day a Friday Journal

Daily Readings from Every Day a Friday

FRESH START

Fresh Start Study Guide

I DECLARE

I Declare Personal Application Guide

NEXT LEVEL THINKING

Next Level Thinking Journal

Next Level Thinking Study Guide

*Daily Readings from Next Level
Thinking*

THE ABUNDANCE MIND-SET

THE POWER OF FAVOR

The Power of Favor Study Guide

THE POWER OF I AM

The Power of I Am Journal

The Power of I Am Study Guide

Daily Readings from The Power of I Am

THINK BETTER, LIVE BETTER

Think Better, Live Better Journal

Think Better, Live Better Study Guide

*Daily Readings from Think Better,
Live Better*

TWO WORDS THAT WILL CHANGE
YOUR LIFE TODAY

WITH VICTORIA OSTEEN

Our Best Life Together

Wake Up to Hope Devotional

YOU CAN, YOU WILL

You Can, You Will Journal

*Daily Readings from You Can,
You Will*

YOUR BEST LIFE NOW

Your Best Life Begins Each Morning

Your Best Life Now for Moms

Your Best Life Now Journal

Your Best Life Now Study Guide

Daily Readings from Your Best Life Now

*Scriptures and Meditations for Your
Best Life Now*

Starting Your Best Life Now

EMPTY OUT THE NEGATIVE

FaithWords
Hachette Book Group
1290 Avenue of the Americas, New York, NY 10104
faithwords.com
twitter.com/faithwords

First Edition: November 2020

FaithWords is a division of Hachette Book Group, Inc. The FaithWords name and logo are trademarks of Hachette Book Group, Inc.

The publisher is not responsible for websites (or their content) that are not owned by the publisher.

The Hachette Speakers Bureau provides a wide range of authors for speaking events. To find out more, go to www.hachettespeakersbureau.com or call (866) 376-6591.

Library of Congress Control Number: 2020941670

ISBN: 978-1-5460-1599-4 (hardcover), 978-1-5460-1600-7 (ebook), 978-1-5460-1604-5 (large print)

Printed in the United States of America

LSC-C

Printing 3, 2021

CONTENTS

CHAPTER ONE

Empty Out the Negative

It's easy to go through life holding on to things that weigh us down—guilt, resentment, doubt, worry. The problem is, when we allow these negative emotions in, they take up space we need for the good things that should be there. Imagine your life is like a container. You were created to be filled with joy, peace, confidence, and creativity. But if you allow worry in, it pushes out the peace. There's not space for both. You can't go above 100-percent capacity; you have a limited amount of space. If you allow guilt to take up space, that's space you don't have for the confidence you need.

The reason some people don't enjoy their lives is because their container, or their heart, is contaminated with so many things. They have 10 percent filled with worry, being stressed out over their job; 12 percent bitterness, being mad at their neighbor; 20 percent guilt, beating themselves up for past mistakes; 9 percent jealousy, thinking their coworker is more beautiful. They don't realize 70 percent of their container is negative. Yet they wonder why they don't have joy, creativity, and passion. They only have room for 30 percent of the good things they should have.

The Scripture says, "Give no place to the enemy." That's not just talking about the forces of darkness. That means to give no place to guilt. Give no place to worry. Give no place to bitterness. Those contaminants can't come in and automatically take over. You control what's in your container. You control what you think about and what you choose to allow in. We all have negative emotions, negative feelings. But you have to make the choice that says, "I'm not going to give this jealousy, this bitterness, or this anger valuable space and let it poison my life. I'm going to protect what I allow in my heart."

Every morning when we wake up, we need to empty out anything negative from the day before. If somebody offended you at work, and

> *You control what's in your container.*
> *You control what you think about and what you choose to allow in.*

they didn't treat you right, it's easy to let that offense stay with you. It can feel good to carry around a grudge. But you have to be disciplined and say, "No, I am not giving this offense any room. I am not going to let it sour my day." That person hurt you once. Don't let that person continue to hurt you by holding on to the offense. Being offended is not harming the other person; it's harming you. It's taking up space you need for the good things that will move you toward your destiny.

Let's say you wake up in the morning and thoughts of worry come. *How are you going to pay your bills? What if the medical report's not good? You'll never get out of this problem.* Don't allow these negative thoughts in. Don't make the mistake of dwelling on them. Just say, "No, thanks. I know God is in control. He has me in the palms of His hands. He'll get me to where I'm supposed to be." Take inventory of what you're giving space to. Life is too short for you to live with negative things holding you down.

Make Room for the Good Things

David says in Psalm 103, "God fills my life with good things so I stay young and strong." I've learned that if you empty out the negative, if you make room, God will fill you with good things. If you empty out the worry, God will fill you with peace. If you empty out the insecurity and the negative things people have said about you, God will fill you with confidence. My question to you is: Is God trying to fill you with good things but there's no room? Is your container full of worry, regret, bitterness, and jealousy? Why don't you start emptying that out? If somebody did you wrong, you could hang on to that bitterness; instead you need to say, "God, I forgive them. I let it go." You didn't just forgive. You made room for God to fill you with good things. That's when He'll give you beauty for ashes and joy for mourning.

Perhaps you're in a tough season. The medical report wasn't good. You should be stressed and worried; instead you say, "God, I trust You. You said You would restore health to me." You just made room for God to fill you with healing. You empty out the worry, and God will give you peace in the midst of the storm.

Perhaps a coworker got the promotion you worked so hard for. Envy and jealousy will come. "I wish that were me. I'm smarter than he is. I don't understand that." Instead of letting that jealousy stay, you need to say, "God, I know You're no respecter of persons. You got the promotion for him, and I know You can do it for me." The good news is, God doesn't run out of

> *Is your container full of worry, regret, bitterness, and jealousy? Why don't you start emptying that out?*

favor. He doesn't have a limited supply. If you empty out the jealousy, then when it's your time to be promoted, God will open doors that no man can shut. If somebody got what you wanted, that simply means it wasn't supposed to be yours. If someone else got the promotion, be happy for that person. God has something better for you. If someone else got the person you wanted to date, don't be upset. God knows what He's doing. If it worked out your way, that person would be second best. The bottom line is, what has your name on it is not going to go to anyone else. Don't go around bitter, with jealousy, in self-pity—that will poison your life. Empty it out. God is in control. He's directing your steps, and at the right time, what has your name on it will show up.

God promises that if we make room, He will not only fill us with good things, but He will keep us young and strong. The reason some people are not young and strong—I don't mean just young physically, but young in spirit, vibrant and passionate about life—is because they're filled with the negative. Worry will make you weak. Living stressed out will make you old, give you wrinkles, and take your passion. Being bitter, angry, and resentful will shorten your life. Proverbs says, "A relaxed attitude lengthens life." You can be eighty years old and young at heart. Your spirit never ages.

I met a woman in the church lobby a while back. It was her hundredth birthday. She was standing there dressed impeccably, looking beautiful, with hardly any wrinkles, and full of joy. Her mind was as sharp as can be. I asked her what her secret was so I could tell Victoria. She said, "I don't worry. I let things go, and I laugh a lot."

> *Living stressed out will make you old, give you wrinkles, and take your passion.*

She's lived by this principle. But you know that in her hundred years, she had troubles, people hurt her, and she made mistakes. Life happened. Offenses came, but she didn't hold on to them. She kept emptying them out, and as God promised, He filled her life with good things and kept her young and strong.

I don't want to get old, grouchy, grumpy, and fall apart. I want to stay young, strong, good-looking, and full of faith, joy, and energy. The way this happens is to give no place to the negative. Get in the habit of emptying out the offenses. Empty out the worry. If you make a mistake, empty out the guilt. If you didn't do your best, empty out the regret. Do better next time. If nobody gave you credit for what you did, empty out the self-pity. If you had a bad break, and you don't understand it, empty out the questions. If you get good at emptying out the negative, you'll be like that woman—strong, young, vibrant, full of faith and full of joy.

Release It

Jesus said, "Blessed are the pure in heart, for they will see God." The word *pure* in the original language is where we get our word *catharsis* from, which means "cleansing, releasing, purifying." If you have surgery, sometimes the doctor will put in a catheter. A catheter is a tube that drains out the impurities in the body, and it comes from the same root word as *catharsis*. A catheter automatically takes what's not beneficial—the toxins, the infections, the waste—and flushes them out of the body. The doctor knows there will be contaminants. He's not alarmed that the body has waste and infection. He's only alarmed when it's not being released, when we're holding on to things that should be flushed out. When God says, "Blessed are the pure in heart," He's saying, "You're going to be blessed when you learn how to release the impurities of life like a catheter does, when you get in a habit of emptying out things that will infect you."

Do you know what bitterness is to our spirit? It's an infection. Guilt is an infection. Worry, doubt, and self-pity are infections. These things are not unusual. Impurities come to us all. But you have to push them out. It's when we hold on to them that they contaminate our spirit and cause us problems. You weren't created to carry around guilt, regret, bitterness, and anger—that poisons your life.

> *Do you know what bitterness is to our spirit? It's an infection.*

"Joel, I'm bitter because I had a bad break." "I'm sour

because somebody walked out on me." I say this respectfully: That's simply an impurity. Why don't you release
it so it doesn't infect the rest of your life? Don't let a disappointment, a divorce, a layoff, or a loss poison your
future. "I'm worried about my health. I'm worried about
my finances. I'm worried about my children." Worry is a
part of life. Those thoughts come to us all. The key is to
not hold on to them. Recognize that they're not beneficial; they're not moving you forward. That's an impurity
that wasn't meant to stay. You have to release it. "God, I
don't see a way, but I know You're still on the throne. I
know You're bigger than this problem. I know You're sup-
plying all my needs." You just released the toxin.

Are you holding on to an infection? To impurities?
Are you angry? Jealous? Worried? Discouraged? Maybe
you had a disappointment, something didn't work out.
Imagine there's an angel who has a delivery package with
your name on it. It says, "Beauty for ashes, new beginnings, new opportunities, and new friendships." He's en
route with those good things. The problem is, if you're
holding on to the old, there's no place for him to deliver

it. I wonder how many things are en route right now. The angel is standing by with our joy, our peace, our confidence, our creativity, or our spouse, but there's no room. Because we're not releasing the toxins—the anger, the bitterness, the jealousy, the worry—he can't deliver those good things. Instead of living blessed and excited about our future, we've become infected. The good news is, you can get rid of that infec-

> *The good news is, you can get rid of that infection. It is not permanent.*

tion. It is not permanent. If you start releasing the regret, the worry, the bitterness, or the anger, it's just a matter of time before that angel shows up with your delivery. When you make room, God promises He will fill your life with good things.

Keep Your Heart Pure

This is what David did. He was an expert at emptying out the negative. As a young man, his family looked down on him and treated him like he was second-class. He could have let that infection take root and lived insecure. Instead, he let it go in one ear and out the other. He knew that if he held on to it, it would keep him from his destiny. Later, David went to the palace and served King Saul faithfully. When Saul was sick, David would play the harp to help him feel better. In return, Saul tried to kill him. Saul was jealous of David, chased him through the desert, and made his life miserable for many years. David could have become bitter and thought, *What's the use? Everybody's against me. Life is not fair.* But instead he kept his heart pure and emptied out the self-pity.

As David did, we all have impurities and infections that come. People come against us for no reason. Our plans don't always work out. It's easy to think, *Why is this happening to me?* It's just life. The Scripture says, "Offenses will come." They're not a problem unless you don't know what to do with them. Too many people make the mistake of holding on to them. They get bitter, live guilty, and get a chip on their shoulder. That's going to poison your future. You have to release the toxins of life. You may not be able to keep them from coming, but you can keep them from staying. David had a pure heart. That means he kept the infections out. It doesn't mean that he was perfect. David made mistakes. He committed adultery and had the woman's husband killed. For one year he tried to cover it up. He was so overwhelmed with guilt and condemnation that he became physically sick and weak. That poison started to infect every part of his life. He finally admitted his mistake. He repented and asked God to forgive him, and things began to turn around. Once he got the infection out, his health was restored.

When you make a mistake, and we all do, don't run away from God. Don't try to hide it. Go to God and repent. That means to not keep doing the same thing. And then ask for forgiveness. Here's the key: You have to receive God's mercy. The enemy is called "the accuser of the brethren." He'll remind you of every mistake you've made for the last thirty years.

It's easy to live your life in regrets, thinking about what you should have done differently. *I should have raised my children better. I should have been more faithful in my marriage. I should have finished college.* Don't go through life looking in the rearview mirror, being down on yourself, living in regrets. You can't do anything about the past, but you can do something about right now. Being against yourself doesn't help you do better; it pushes you down. The moment you asked God to forgive you, He forgave you. Why don't you forgive yourself? Why don't you empty out the guilt? Why don't you turn off the accusing voices? The Scripture says God doesn't remember your mistakes anymore. If someone is bringing up the negative things of your past, it's not God; that's the accuser trying to deceive you into living condemned.

> *Don't go through life looking in the rearview mirror, being down on yourself, living in regrets.*

Unforgiveness Is Like a Poisonous Toxin

How much space are you giving to guilt, to shame, to regret, to being against yourself? Whatever it is, it's too much. You need that space for the good things God has for you that will move you toward your destiny. If you're giving space to guilt, you will not have the confidence you need to move forward, which will cause you to fail again. It's a negative cycle. The only way to break the cycle is to rise up and say, "That's it. I am done living in the past, focused on my mistakes, reliving my failures, and beating myself up. This is a new day. I'm emptying out all that infection. I'm going to receive God's mercy." You have to do this by faith, because every voice will tell you that you're a hypocrite. "God's not going to forgive you. Look what you've done." It doesn't have anything to do with what you have or haven't done. It has to do with what Jesus has already done.

"Joel, I've made a lot of mistakes. I don't deserve to be blessed." None of us deserve it. This is what mercy is all about. That's why it's called the "Good News." Your sins have already been forgiven. You don't have to pay God back for your mistakes, because the price has already been paid. When you fall, don't stay down; get back up. When the accuser whispers, "Look at you. You blew it again. You'll never get it right," just answer back, "Yes, I know I'm not perfect, but I am forgiven. I may not be where I should be, but I'm making progress. I'm moving forward. I'm not where I used to be." Don't let guilt poison your future. Empty it out.

Sometimes it's hard to empty out the negative. When a person does us wrong, our human nature wants to hold on to the hurt, to become bitter, and carry around a grudge. We think, *I'm not going to forgive them. They don't deserve it.* But you're not forgiving for their sake; you're forgiving for your sake. As long as you hold on to the hurt, the anger, and the bitterness, it's not affecting the other person; it's infecting you. Unforgiveness is like a poisonous toxin. It may feel good to hold on to it, but it will contaminate your life. However, I realize there are times that the right kind of anger is necessary, but what I want you to watch out for is negative anger.

> As long as you hold on to the hurt, the anger, and the bitterness, it's not affecting the other person; it's infecting you.

Oftentimes the reason we don't forgive is because what the other person did was wrong. They were clearly at fault. But when you forgive, you're not excusing their behavior. You're not lessening the offense; you're simply getting the poison out of you. You have to forgive so you can be free. Quit looking at it as though you're doing them a favor. You're doing yourself a favor, because it takes a lot of emotional energy to hold a grudge, to live with unforgiveness. You wake up, and it's always on your mind; you're thinking about how someone did you wrong. You may not realize it, but you are spending emotional energy that you need for your dreams, for your goals, for your children. You won't become all you were created to be if you are wasting emotional energy on things that don't matter. That unforgiveness is an impurity. Yes, what they did was wrong, but you have to let it pass. You have to release it. When you do, you'll not only feel a new freedom and have more energy, but God will be your vindicator. He will make your wrongs right. You don't have to pay people back. You're not the judge; God is. Leave it up to Him, and He'll vindicate you better than you can vindicate yourself.

Just Get Past It

This is what Mary Johnson did. Mary is a single mother of one son. When her son was twenty years old, he was out late one night at a party when he was approached by a sixteen-year-old boy named Oshea Israel, whom he had never met before. Oshea had been drinking, and there was an altercation between them. In the heat of the moment, Oshea pulled out a gun and murdered Mary's only son. She was so filled with anger and hatred that she told the judge that Oshea was an animal who needed to be caged. When he was only charged with second-degree murder, Mary was even angrier. She became a recluse, stayed in her house, and wouldn't look at her son's picture. Ten years passed.

Finally, Mary knew it was time to forgive. She could hear the still small voice telling her to let it go. She contacted the prison to see if she could visit Oshea. They said yes, but Oshea said no. He wouldn't do it. She kept asking and asking, and finally he agreed. When she came into the prison and saw Oshea, he gave her a big hug and held on to her. They wept and wept. Mary said, "As I was embracing Oshea, I could feel hatred and bitterness rising up out of me and leaving my body." It was so strong that she fell over, and Oshea had to hold her up. That day, Mary not only emptied out the unforgiveness, but she found a new son. Seven

> *She could hear the still small voice telling her to let it go.*

years later, Oshea was released on parole and didn't have any place to live. Mary said, "You can live next door to me." She calls him her "spiritual son." Mary started an organization called "From Death to Life" to help bring healing and reconciliation between families of victims and those who have caused harm. Now she and Oshea go out together and speak at conferences and schools about forgiveness and overcoming loss.

Mary Johnson said what really helped her decide

to forgive was a poem she read about two mothers in Heaven who had just become friends. One mother asked the other, "Who is your son?" She replied, "My son is Jesus. I'm Mary." Then Mary asked, "Who is your son?" The other mother answered, "My son is Judas." Hearing how Mary, the mother of Christ, had befriended the mother of Judas, and how they shared a common pain, Mary Johnson knew she had to reach out to Oshea's family. Now she helps other mothers do the same thing. Out of your pain can come your purpose.

I saw a lady on television whose son had been killed in an accident many years earlier. They asked her how she was doing, and she made this statement: "You never really get over it, but you can get past it." She was saying, "Yes, it's difficult. Yes, there was a season of mourning, but you don't have to stay in mourning. You don't have to live bitter. You don't have to get stuck in grief or depression. You can move forward."

When you go through a loss, things happen that you don't understand, and it's easy to think, *I just need to get over this*. But sometimes that's too strong. It can put more

Empty Out the Negative   21

pressure on us. We think, *Why do I feel this way? I must be doing something wrong.* Take the pressure off. You don't have to get over it; just get past it. Just keep moving forward, taking it one day at a time. God said that He will never give you something that you cannot handle. You may not understand why it happened, but the Scripture says, "God will give us a peace that passes understanding." You're not going to figure everything out. If you let go of the questions of life, you will have a peace that goes beyond what you can understand.

All the "Littles" Add Up to a Lot

Toward the end of Jesus' life, He'd been betrayed by one of His disciples, mocked by the soldiers, and falsely accused of crimes. Now He was hanging on the cross, wearing a crown of thorns, about to breathe His last breath, when He did something significant. He could have just died and gone on to Heaven, and that was it. Instead, He said, "Father, before I go, I need to take care of one last thing: Forgive them, for they know not what they do." The religious leaders and Roman soldiers didn't ask for forgiveness. They didn't deserve it. Jesus was saying, "I'm not going to leave this earth with anything negative in Me." He was showing us by example how we should release the toxins, release the impurities.

> *Jesus was saying, "I'm not going to leave this earth with anything negative in Me." He was showing us by example how we should release the toxins, release the impurities.*

There is an old legend about Leonardo da Vinci. The legend says that when da Vinci was painting the portrait of Christ in his mural of the Last Supper, he could not make any progress as he tried to paint the face of Christ. The legend goes on to say that da Vinci finally realized that until he forgave another person for whom he held hatred in his heart, he could not complete his masterpiece. That's what happens when we hold on to negatives. It stifles our creativity. We don't do our best work. It's because there's infection that's slowing us down.

Are you allowing negative things into your container? To reach the fullness of your destiny, you need to operate at your maximum potential. If you have a little bitterness, a little guilt, a little jealousy, plus a little worry in your heart, all the spaces of those "littles" add up to a lot, and you end up only operating at a fraction of what you could. I'm asking you to empty all that out. God is ready to fill your life with good things. He wants to keep you young and strong. Do your part and make room for Him. Every morning, empty out the guilt, empty out the worry, empty out the discouragement. And when the impurities come, when the infection comes, don't let it stay. Let it pass on through. Keep your heart pure. If you do this, you're going to step up to a new level with more joy, more peace, and more favor.

CHAPTER TWO

Power Thinking

It's easy to go around thinking that the obstacle is too big, that we'll never get well, that a virus or an illness is going to get the best of us. We wonder why we don't have any strength and why we can't get ahead. It's because our thoughts are limiting us. We draw in what we constantly think about. You can't think defeat and have victory. You can't think weak and have strength. You can't think *not able to* and accomplish your dreams. Your life is going to follow your thoughts. Instead of thinking weak, defeated, not-able-to thoughts, you need to start thinking power thoughts. *This sickness is no match for me. No virus can stop my destiny. This trouble at work is not how my story ends. The forces for me are greater than the forces against me.* Victory starts in our minds. Success, breakthroughs, and new levels depend on our thinking.

"Joel, the threat of a pandemic has me afraid. I'm worried about my finances. I'm stressed over my children." That's drawing in more negativity. That's making you weaker, draining your strength, your energy, and your passion. You'll be amazed at what will happen if you start thinking power thoughts. *No weapon formed against me will prosper. God has me in the palms of His hands. He's the guardian of my soul. He has made me untouchable to the enemy.* When you dwell on these thoughts, you'll feel strength rising up, courage and determination. This is not just being positive; this is your faith being released.

The writer of Proverbs says, "Be careful what you think, because your thoughts run your life." Are your thoughts helping you or hurting you? Are you thinking power thoughts, victory thoughts, what I call "well-able" thoughts, or are you thinking defeated thoughts such as,

I'll never get well, never accomplish my dreams, never break this addiction? You're choosing the direction your life is going to go. Pay attention to what your mind is dwelling on. Don't just think any thought that comes to mind. If it's a negative, discouraging, fearful thought, don't give it the time of day. Turn it around and dwell on what God says about you. Thoughts will whisper, *Nothing good is in your future. You've seen your best days.* If you dwell on that you'll miss your destiny. Tune out that defeated thought and think power thoughts. *Something good is going to happen to me. Favor is surrounding me like a shield. Goodness and mercy are following me.*

> *Are your thoughts helping you or hurting you?*

When you're in tough times, the enemy will work overtime trying to convince you that the problem is too big, that you'll never get out of debt, that your child will never turn around. He knows that if he can keep you defeated in your thoughts, he'll keep you defeated in your life. The battle is taking place in your mind. Thoughts will tell you, *It's never going to change. You can't take it anymore. Just give up on that dream.* Instead of thinking those weak thoughts, drawing in more weakness, turn it around and think power thoughts. *Yes, this problem is big, but I've been armed with strength for every battle. I am full of can-do power. What God started in my life, He will finish. This difficulty didn't come to stay; it came to pass.* God says He will never let you face anything that you can't handle. He will always give you the grace, the strength, and the faith for what comes your way. But if you're believing those lies that it's too much, you're going to feel overwhelmed. If you're dwelling on weak, limiting, can't-do-it thoughts, you'll get stuck where you are. Pay attention to what's going on in your mind.

Victory Is Already Promised

This is what happened to the Israelites when Moses sent twelve men to spy out the Promised Land. After forty days, ten spies came back and said, "Moses, we'll never defeat them. The people are huge. They looked like giants. We don't have a chance." God had already promised them the victory. He had already said that this was their land, but notice what they were thinking—weak, defeated, limiting, fearful thoughts. The other two spies, Joshua and Caleb, came back with a different report. They said, "Moses, we are well able to take the land. Yes, the people are big, but we know our God is bigger. Let us go in at once and take it." What's interesting is that they saw the same giants as the other ten spies. Joshua and Caleb saw the same problems, the same opposition, the same land, but instead of thinking defeated thoughts, they chose to think power thoughts. They weren't any bigger than the other spies, and they didn't have more training, more experience, or more weapons. The only difference was their thinking.

> *Joshua and Caleb saw the same problems, the same opposition, the same land, but instead of thinking defeated thoughts, they chose to think power thoughts.*

The negative report from the ten spies began to spread throughout the Israelite camp. Before long all two million people who had escaped slavery in Egypt were afraid and worried. They said, "Moses, let's go back to Egypt. Let's go back to being slaves." That's how powerful our thoughts are. Ten men infected the rest of the people, and they ended up wandering in the desert for the next forty years. Be careful how you think. Don't get infected and miss your destiny. Are you one of the ten spies? "I can't beat this illness. I can't accomplish my dream. I don't have the connections. I had this big setback at work that's going to ruin my business." None of the challenges you are facing is a surprise to God. You wouldn't be facing it if you couldn't handle it. As with the Israelites, He has already promised you the victory.

The apostle Paul says, "Thanks be to God who always causes us to triumph." He didn't say some of the time, or most of the time; he said *always*, all of the time. It may be tough now, but keep the right perspective. Victory is in your future. Healing is in your future, abundance is in your future, and freedom is in your future. The giants may be big, but our God is bigger. The obstacle may be high, but our God is the Most High. A virus may be powerful, but our God is all-powerful. I'm asking you to be a Joshua, be a Caleb. Think power thoughts, think can-do thoughts, think victory thoughts. Don't look at how big the problem is; look at how big your God is. He parted the Red Sea, He closed the mouths of lions, and He brought the dead back to life. That obstacle is no match for Him. He didn't bring you this far to leave you. When you believe, all things are possible. Get your thoughts going in the right direction.

The Scripture says, "When the enemy comes in like a flood, the Spirit of the Lord will raise up a barrier against him." You're not fighting this battle on your own. The most powerful force in the universe is fighting for you, pushing back forces of darkness, keeping that sickness from taking you out, moving the wrong people out of the way, opening doors that no man can shut. All through the day you need to

> *Don't look at how big the problem is; look at how big your God is.*

say, "I am well able. I have can-do power. I will overcome this obstacle. I will defeat this sickness. I will rise out of lack and struggle. I will accomplish my dreams." When you think and speak like that, the Creator of the universe goes to work, and miracles are set in motion.

Don't Think Like Everyone Else Does

It's significant that ten spies were negative and two were positive. It's about the same today. Eighty percent of people will be negative, and twenty percent will be positive. Eighty percent will focus on how big the problem is and live afraid. They'll tell you how you won't get well, and how you should just settle where you are. If you're going to fulfill your destiny, you have to go against the grain. You can't just fit in and be afraid like most people, or complain like your coworkers, or be negative like your neighbor. God is looking for Joshuas. He's looking for Calebs. He's looking for people who stand out. He's looking for people who believe when it seems impossible, and who aren't discouraged by how big the opposition is.

If this is going to happen, you have to guard your

mind, because negative news spreads faster than good news. Joshua and Caleb said, "We are well able." That news didn't go anywhere. When people heard that the giants were too big, that they didn't have a chance, that news spread like wildfire throughout the camp. Negative thinking is contagious. All around us there's negative news, with analysts telling us how bad the sickness is, how bad the economy is, what might happen, and how it can get much worse. I'm not faulting them; they're doing their job. It's good to be informed, but you can't let that poison stay in your spirit. If you keep dwelling on that, you're going to end up afraid, worried, panicked, and thinking you're not going to make it. When you dwell on negative thoughts, it becomes a cycle that keeps drawing in more fear, more worry, and more defeat.

The prophet Isaiah says, "Do not think like everyone else does. Don't be afraid that some plan conceived behind closed doors will be the end of you. Do not fear anything except the Lord Almighty. If you fear Him, you

> *Negative thinking is contagious.*

need fear nothing else. He will keep you safe." You don't have to fear a virus, or fear what the economy is going to do, or fear the future. Just keep honoring God, and He will keep you safe. He'll defeat your enemies. He'll do what medicine can't do. He'll turn your child around. He'll free you from that addiction.

God says you should not think like everyone else does. Don't think like the ten spies. When the majority are afraid, worried, and negative, you have to be on the offensive and say, "No, I'm not falling into that trap. I'm not going to think weak, defeated thoughts. I'm going to think power thoughts. I know that my God is still on the throne. I know that His being for me is more than the world being against me. I am well able to accomplish my dream. I will defeat this addiction. I will outlast this opposition. I have strength for all things."

Out of those two million people, the only ones who ever made it into the Promised Land were Joshua and Caleb. It's not a coincidence that they were the only ones who thought power thoughts. You can't reach your destiny thinking negative, limiting thoughts.

Power Up Your Mind

I have a bike path that I like to travel often. The route takes about an hour, and most of it is flat, but there's one very big hill. Making it up that hill requires digging down deep and really pushing. I like to exercise, and I always get prepared mentally for this hill and enjoy the challenge. But on one particular day I was tired. I had worked out hard a couple of days before, and I had been traveling a lot and had not gotten much sleep. About ten minutes into my ride, I started thinking, *I don't want to go up that hill. I don't feel like it. I don't have the strength. I don't want to have to push.* I kept dreading it, telling myself over and over how hard it was going to be, wondering if I could make it. But at one point I received a phone call, put it on speaker, and started talking. As I was riding, we talked and talked. About twenty minutes later, I hung up.

I went right back to thinking about my bike ride. *Okay, I don't want to go up that hill.* But when I looked around, I realized that I had already gone up the hill. I had ridden up it while I was talking, but because I was distracted, not thinking about how hard it was going to be, not convincing myself that I couldn't do it, I made it up the hill with no problem. My legs weren't burning, and I wasn't winded. I didn't feel any more tired than before. I don't even remember going up it. I wonder how many things we're telling ourselves that we can't do are just like that hill. "I can't deal with these unfair people at work. I can't handle this challenge in my health. I can't lose this weight." We're dreading things, thinking weak, defeated thoughts, when the truth is that we've already been equipped to handle it. We have the strength for all things.

When God created you, He put in you everything you need to fulfill your destiny. Now quit telling yourself what you can't do and how it's not going to work out. All that's doing is draining your strength. When you get to that hill, you're going to discover that it's easier than you thought. You're going to have strength that you didn't know you had. It's like when your car is going up a hill and the extra cylinders kick in to give you more power. When you need it, God's grace is going to kick in and help you do what you didn't think you could do. The key is: Don't cancel out the strength with weak thinking.

Every morning when you wake up, you need to power up and get your mind going in the right direction. *This is going to be a good day. I can handle anything that comes my way. I am strong. I am confident. I have the favor of God. Angels are watching over me. I'm excited about my future.* Set your mind for victory at the beginning of each day. Don't let just any thoughts play. You have to think thoughts on purpose. If you wake up and just think whatever comes to mind, thoughts will tell you, *You have too many problems. You're too tired. You'll never overcome this obstacle. Nothing good is going to happen today.* If you don't set the tone for the day, negative thoughts will set it for you. Before you check your phone, before you read your email, before you see what the weather is like, you need to think power

> *If you don't set the tone for the day, negative thoughts will set it for you.*

thoughts—victory thoughts, abundance thoughts, can-do thoughts—on purpose.

Get in Tune

Psalm 125 says, "God will be good to those whose hearts are in tune with Him." Notice that you can be in tune or out of tune with God. The way you get in tune is by thinking victorious, overcoming, faith-filled thoughts. If you go around thinking, *I'll never get well. This depression, or this anxiety, or this addiction is going to hinder me all my life,* unfortunately, you're not in tune with God. You can't find anywhere in the Scripture where God says, "I'm weak. I'm discouraged. I'm afraid. The enemy is getting the best of me." God says, "I am all-powerful. I spoke worlds into existence. I flung stars into space." When Moses asked God what His name is, He answered, "My name is I AM." He was saying, "I am everything. I am strength. I am healing. I am provision. I am abundance. I am protection. I am favor." When God said, "Let there be light," it came at 186,000 miles per second. One angel in the Old Testament destroyed 185,000 soldiers in an army of Israel's enemies. If you're going to get in tune with God, you can't think little, weak, defeated, get-by, hope-this-works-out thoughts. You have to think bold thoughts, favor thoughts, abundance thoughts, healing thoughts, victorious thoughts.

The opposition may be much bigger and stronger. Just agree with what God says. "Lord, You say that when the enemy comes against me one way, You will defeat them and cause them to flee seven different ways." When thoughts tell you, *You'll never get well*, get in tune with God and say, "Lord, thank You that You are restoring health to me. Thank You that the number of my days, You will fulfill." If the thought comes, *This setback has ruined my year financially. Just accept it and wait for next year*, you need to respond, "Lord, thank You that the economy is not my source. You are my source. You said You would make rivers in the deserts and streams in the barren places." When you have the thought, *You'll never have a baby. You heard the experts. It's not possible*, you say, "Father, You say that what's impossible with people is possible with God. You say You will make the barren woman to be a happy mother of children. So, Father, thank You that my baby is on the way."

The way to get in tune with God is to think what He says about you—not what you feel, not what it looks like, not what the experts say, and not what the economy says. Get in tune with what the Most High God has spoken over you. The Scripture says, "Whose report will you believe?" Will you believe what the ten spies are saying, the negative report telling you what you can't do and how it's too tough? Or will you believe what Joshua and Caleb are saying, how you are well able?

> *The way to get in tune with God is to think what He says about you.*

Who Told You That?

When my father went to be with the Lord and I stepped up to pastor the church, every thought told me that I

couldn't do it. I wasn't qualified. I didn't have the training. I was too quiet. If I had believed that report, I would
have missed my destiny. That's why the Scripture says,
"Be careful what you think." It gives us a warning. Your
thoughts set the limits for your life. All that came to my
mind were negative, fearful, intimidating thoughts. I had
to do what I'm asking you to do. I didn't just keep thinking those thoughts because they showed up. I didn't dwell
on them and believe they were the truth. I tuned them
out and got in tune with God. On purpose I thought, *I
can do all things through Christ. I am strong in the Lord.
I've been raised up for such a time as this. Father, thank You
that I'm equipped, empowered, and anointed.*

Thoughts told me, *Nobody's going to listen to you,
Joel. You don't have anything to say.* Instead of believing
those lies, I would say, "Father, thank You that Your favor
is causing me to stand out. Thank You that people are
going to like me and be drawn to me. When they see me
on the television or radio or Internet, they can't turn me
off." If I had not gotten in tune with God and thought
these power thoughts, I wouldn't be where I am today.

When Adam and Eve were in the Garden of Eden, they ate the fruit that God told them not to eat, and then they ran and hid. God came looking for them and said, "Adam, where are you?" Adam answered, "We're hiding, because we're naked." God replied, "Adam, who told you that you were naked?" God knew that the enemy had been talking to him. God is saying to you, "Who told you that you're not qualified? Who told you that you've made too many mistakes? Who told you that you come from the wrong family, and you'll never be successful?" Those are the wrong voices to listen to. Tune them out and get in tune with God. When thoughts tell you, *You're just average. There's nothing special about you*, get rid of those defeated thoughts and think power thoughts. *I am fearfully and wonderfully made. I am a masterpiece. I have royal blood flowing through my veins. I am crowned with favor. I will leave my mark.* If you get in tune with God, He'll open doors no person can shut. He'll take you where you can't go on your own.

> *If you get in tune with God, He'll open doors no person can shut.*

When thoughts tell you, *You've been through too much.* *You lost a loved one. The business didn't make it. Your friend* *walked out on you. Nothing good is in your future*, don't believe those lies. Get in tune with God and say, "Father, thank You that You have beauty for these ashes. Thank You that what was meant for my harm, You're turning to my advantage." When you're in tune with God, He'll pay you back for the wrongs. The prophet Isaiah says, "He will give you double for the unfair things that happened." Instead of thinking you've seen your best days, you can say, "Lord, thank You that double is coming. Thank You that my latter days will be better than my former days."

Get Rid of Any Dead-Dog Thinking

In the Scripture, there was a young man named Mephibosheth, who was the grandson of King Saul and the son of Jonathan, David's best friend. Mephibosheth was born into royalty, destined to one day take the throne. But at five years old, his grandfather and father were killed in battle. When word reached the palace, the nurse who took care of him picked him up and took off running, afraid that the enemy army was coming to kill him. In her haste, she accidentally dropped Mephibosheth, injuring both of his legs. He became crippled for life. Sometimes well-meaning people can drop you. This nurse had good intentions, was trying to help him, but she dropped him. Years passed, and Mephibosheth ended up living in exile in a city called Lo Debar, one of the poorest, most run-down cities of that day. The name *Lo Debar* means "without pasture." It was like a wasteland, with no greenery, no place to grow crops. Mephibosheth, the grandson of the king, who had royalty in his blood and had lived in the palace, was now living in the slums, barely surviving.

One day King David was thinking about his friend Jonathan. He asked his men if any of Jonathan's relatives were still alive so he could be good to them. A former servant of the house of Saul came and told David about Mephibosheth. David's men went and searched through the slums of Lo Debar and finally found Mephibosheth, who was now a grown man. They had to carry him back to David's palace. I'm sure that Mephibosheth was afraid, thinking that David was going to punish him or kill him because his grandfather, King Saul, had tried to kill David, but it was just the opposite. David was incredibly kind to him. He said, "From now on, you're going to live in the palace with me. Every night, you're going to have dinner at my table. I'm going to restore to you all the land that belonged to your grandfather, King Saul." Mephibosheth was overwhelmed. He couldn't believe what was happening. But the way he responded to David's kindness shows why he was living in Lo Debar all those years. He said to David, "Why would you be so kind to such a dead dog as I?" Notice his weak, defeated thoughts, saying, "I don't deserve to be blessed. I've had too many bad breaks. People dropped me."

I wonder how many of us are doing as Mephibosheth did. We are sons and daughters of the Most High God. We have royalty in our blood, and we're destined to reign in life. But because we've been dropped—somebody did us wrong, we went through disappointments, things that weren't fair—now we're living in Lo Debar, thinking we don't deserve to be blessed. Or because we made mistakes, got off course, and brought trouble on ourselves, we're thinking we just have to sit on the sidelines, make it through life, and accept that our dreams will never come to pass. Can I encourage you to get rid of that dead-dog thinking? Nothing that's happened to you has to keep you from your destiny. You may have had some bad breaks, but that didn't stop God's plan for your life.

Now you have to do your part. Quit thinking limited, defeated, unworthy thoughts, and start thinking victory thoughts, abundance thoughts, favor thoughts. Put your shoulders back, hold your head high, and remember who you are and whose you are—a child of the Most High. Get in tune with

> *I wonder how many of us are doing as Mephibosheth did.*

Him. Like David's men who went searching through Lo Debar, God is looking for you today. He's saying, "I'm about to do a new thing. I'm about to pay you back for the wrongs. I'm about to open new doors and turn negative situations around." As with Mephibosheth, you're going to be amazed at the goodness of God.

What Are You Thinking About?

I'm asking you to pay attention to what you're thinking about. You are drawing in what you're constantly dwelling on. Your thoughts are running your life. Is what you're thinking about what you want? Are you thinking weak, defeated, "I can't do it" thoughts, or are you thinking power thoughts, such as, *I am well able. God is fighting my battles. Something good is in my future*? Don't be like the ten spies, the 80 percent who are negative. Stand out

> *Is what you're thinking about what you want?*

in the crowd. Be a Joshua, be a Caleb, and think victory thoughts. If you do this, I believe and declare that like Joshua and Caleb, you're going to make it into your Promised Land. You're going to see God show out in your life. Like with Mephibosheth, everything you've lost, God is about to restore. The health, the finances, and the dreams are going to come looking for you.

CHAPTER THREE

A Fresh New Attitude

Studies show that your attitude will have a greater impact on your success in life than your IQ. You can be extremely talented and have incredible potential, but a bad attitude will keep you from rising higher. We spend so much time and money making sure our outside looks good—eating healthy, working out, wearing the latest fashion. That's all fine, but too often we're not spending any time on what's inside. Nice clothes won't cover up a sour attitude. A beautiful face can't hide being bitter inside.

When I was in high school, there was a new girl who moved into town and joined our class. She was so beautiful, a knockout. I was so shy that I didn't ever have the nerve to talk to her. I just admired her from a distance. During my senior year, I had a class with her. Our seating was assigned, and it just so happened that I was sitting right next to her. I thought I had died and gone to Heaven. The first time I sat down by her, I turned toward her and said hello, just being friendly, nothing more. She looked at me as though I had just insulted her and she was totally offended. She turned away, put her nose up in the air, and never said a word to me the whole semester. She was beautiful outside, but to be honest, she was ugly inside. I never saw her the same way. A bad attitude makes you unattractive. It overrides what's outside. It's important to look good and develop our talents, to get a good education, and to stay in shape, but it's more important to keep a good attitude. Nobody wants to be around a sour, critical, condescending person.

The apostle Paul says, "Dress in the wardrobe God picked out for you: kindness and compassion." As a parent, sometimes you pick out clothes for your children to wear. Our heavenly Father has picked out something for all of us to wear—kindness, being good to people, being pleasant to be around. When you're kind, you draw people to you. When you're good-natured and friendly, opportunities will come your way. People want to do business with people they like and can depend upon. When we're hiring someone, their résumé tells us what they can do, what their skills are, their education, and their work history. But we always meet with them because we want to evaluate their attitude. Are they positive, friendly, kind, and considerate? We can find someone else with similar skills and background. The real question is, do they have the attitude that's going to take us higher? They can be gifted, but a negative attitude will pull the team down. Your attitude can make up for a lack of experience, a lack of training, and a lack of talent.

> *Your attitude can make up for a lack of experience, a lack of training, and a lack of talent.*

"Joel, I've always been a bit negative, sarcastic, and condescending. That's just who I am." No, that's who you're choosing to be. That's not who you are. Maybe that's how you were raised, that's what you saw modeled as you grew up, but that's not how you have to stay. Try being kind, considerate, and pleasant to be around. You'll not only enjoy life more, but you'll go further and people will treat you better.

Check Your Attitude Indicator

In an airplane cockpit there's an instrument called an attitude indicator. It shows how level the plane is oriented to the earth's horizon. If the pilot wants to ascend, he puts the plane nose high, and if he wants to descend, he puts the plane nose down. It's the same principle in life. If you have a nose-high attitude, if you're positive—you see the best, you're good to people, you have a smile, you've made up your mind to enjoy the day—you're going to keep rising higher. You're going to see God's goodness and favor. But if you're sour—you don't want to go to work, you're hard to get along with, you're bitter over disappointments—because your attitude is nose down, you're going to go that direction. Sometimes we're discouraged because of what we've brought on ourselves. It's not the enemy; it's our attitude.

The good news is that all you have to do is make an attitude adjustment. It's not complicated. You can't change other people, and you can't change your circumstances, or how you were raised, or who your parents are, but you can change your attitude. There are a lot of things we have no control over. The one thing you can always control is your attitude. Am I going to live this day sour, discouraged, and with a chip on my shoulder, or am I going to live in faith, hopeful, kind, happy, and seeing the best? This is a decision we must make each day. If you're going to have a good attitude, you have to do it on purpose, because all kinds of negative things will try to creep in—discouragement, self-pity, bitterness. If you're not proactive and don't choose to have the right attitude, the wrong attitude will show up.

When a pilot makes a small tweak and tilts the airplane's nose just a little higher, the plane will have climbed thousands of feet in half an hour. I wonder what would happen in your life if you made a small attitude tweak. Instead of going to work sour, dreading the day, and feeling unappreciated, what would happen if you showed up with a smile, being grateful that you have the position, knowing that you're not working unto people and that God is keeping the records? That's what allows God to change things. What would happen

> *If you're not proactive and don't choose to have the right attitude, the wrong attitude will show up.*

in your marriage if you made a small attitude adjustment? Instead of being condescending and hard to get along with, what if you start being kind, loving, and considerate? What if instead of saying hurtful, critical things, you bite your tongue? What if you start giving compliments, telling your spouse how much you love them and how blessed you are to have them? Just a simple tweak, getting your attitude higher, and watch how your relationships will start to improve.

Maybe you've had bad breaks, and life hasn't treated

you fairly. It's easy to live bitter, have a chip on your shoulder, and be focused on the wrongs—that's a nose-down attitude. You're setting the direction you want to go. Why don't you go nose up? *It wasn't fair, but I know God is my vindicator. God is fighting my battles. He promised to pay me back double. I'm expecting favor in great ways.* You keep that attitude up, and you'll see God make up for the wrongs.

A Fresh Mental and Spiritual Attitude

This is what Joseph did. He was betrayed by his brothers, sold into slavery in Egypt, falsely accused of a crime, and put in prison. For many years he was mistreated. It wasn't fair. He was doing the right thing, but the wrong thing kept happening. Yet you never read that Joseph complained, that he got bitter, or that he started slacking off. Despite all the injustice, he kept his attitude nose high. He kept doing the right thing, he kept being good to people, and he kept thanking God that He was in control. Thirteen years later, God vindicated him and made him the prime minister of Egypt. What you're going through may not be fair. People may not be treating you right. It would be easy to get discouraged and live sour. It's a test. God is seeing what you are going to do in the difficult times. Too many people go nose down, and their attitude keeps them from seeing justice and vindication. If you do as Joseph did and stay nose high, you'll keep doing the right thing, keep being good to people who are not good to you, keep a smile, and keep a song of praise. That's not just being positive; that's an attitude of faith, that's what allows God to show out in your life.

The Scripture says, "Put on a garment of praise for a spirit of heaviness." A garment is like a coat. Before you can put on a coat of praise, you have to take off a coat of heaviness. Sometimes we wonder why we don't have any joy, why we're not passionate. We're wearing the wrong coat. *Nothing good is in my future. I never get any breaks.* Let me give you a fashion tip. That coat of discouragement doesn't look good on you. That coat of self-pity is out of style. That coat of bitterness over who left you and what you didn't get doesn't fit you anymore. It's restricting you from coming into a new season. Now do your part and take off that old coat of heaviness. Take off that coat of offense and put on a coat of praise. "Father, thank

> *Sometimes we wonder why we don't have any joy, why we're not passionate. We're wearing the wrong coat.*

You that Your plans for me are for good. Thank You that what You started in my life You will finish." If you're going to go up like a plane, you have to get your nose up, you have to adjust your attitude. You can't have a defeated mentality and live a victorious life.

The apostle Paul wrote to the believers in Ephesus, "Be constantly renewed in the spirit of your mind, putting on a fresh mental and spiritual attitude." He was saying that every day you need to put on a fresh new attitude, because yesterday's attitude will get old. If you don't start afresh and anew, you'll bring all the negative from yesterday into today. If you do that week after week, month after month, before long you'll be critical, negative, seeing the worst. *I don't like my job. This traffic is terrible. My house is too small. I'll never get well.* You know what that is—an old attitude. Some people haven't put on a new attitude for years. They wonder why everything is a burden, why it's so heavy. It's their attitude.

When you wake up each morning, you need to say, "Father, thank You for this day. Thank You that You woke me up and gave me air to breathe. Thank You that You've surrounded me with favor. Everything may not be perfect, but I know that You're on the throne. I am grateful to be alive. I'm grateful for my family. I'm grateful for the opportunities, and I'm going to make the most of this day." That's putting on a fresh new attitude. You wipe the slate clean. Let go of the disappointments of yesterday, let go of what didn't work out, and get your mind going in the right direction. "I'm going to see the good today. I'm going to be kind to others. I'm going to stay in faith and enjoy this day."

Don't Wait to Change

Imagine if you didn't change your clothes for thirty years—that you wore the same clothes and never washed them. They would be dirty and would stink. Nobody would want to be around you. It's the same way with our attitude. An old attitude will drive people away. A sour attitude will keep you from being promoted. A stinking attitude will stop your dreams from coming to pass.

I know a man who was always finding fault with his employer. He constantly challenged the company's policies and bucked the system. The management was good to him, and everyone else in his department loved the company. But he always found something to complain about. For instance, the company policy was that employees had to be at work at eight in the morning. His attitude was that if he was on the company's property at eight o'clock, as in parking his car in the big garage before the long walk to his office, that meant he was on time, and they couldn't do anything about it. That's not what anyone else thought, but he kept doing it his own way, being contentious. After several years, he was let go and lost a prominent position.

This man went to work for another company and did the same thing. He kept challenging the policies, being hard to get along with. One day he was not only fired, but security was called to escort him out of the building and he was told that he wasn't allowed back on the property. What am I saying? A bad attitude will follow you around. We can change jobs, thinking other people are the problem, but sometimes we have to look inside and see if we're the problem. *Do I have a sour attitude, am I being hard to get along with, am I focused on the negative, being critical, finding fault?* This man was talented,

> A bad attitude will follow you around.

smart, and had a big future in front of him, but he lived nose down. His attitude took him in the wrong direction. With a simple adjustment, his story would be different. He would be at another level.

What direction is your attitude taking you? In your

marriage, are you kind, loving, and fun to be around? In your career, are you positive, being your best, helping others? Or do you need to make an adjustment? Don't wait until something big happens—the relationship ends, the company says it doesn't need you, the team says you're not helping them move forward. Make the change now. Get rid of anything that's weighing you down—being sarcastic, condescending, finding fault. That old attitude doesn't smell good. It's going to taint you everywhere you go.

Is Your Window Clean?

There was a couple that moved into a new neighborhood. One morning while they were eating breakfast, the wife looked out the window and saw her neighbor hanging the wash on the line to dry. She noticed the wash was dingy and dirty and said to her husband, "That lady doesn't know how to do laundry. Her clothes aren't clean. I wonder if she even uses detergent." Day after day went by, and the wife made the same comment. "I can't believe that lady doesn't know how to wash." A few weeks later, she looked out the window and the lady's clothes were as clean and bright as could be. She was so surprised that she called to her husband and said, "Look! She finally learned how to wash. I wonder what happened?" The husband smiled and said, "Honey, I got up early this morning and cleaned our window." The problem wasn't that the other lady had dirty laundry; the problem was the window she was looking out wasn't clean.

How dirty the neighbor's clothes are depends on how clean your window is. The Scripture says, "To the pure all things are pure." If you're always finding fault, complaining about the traffic, critical of your spouse, and focused on what's not working out, may I suggest that your window is dirty. The problem is not external; it's internal. You're looking through a tainted

> If you're always finding fault, complaining about the traffic, critical of your spouse, and focused on what's not working out, may I suggest that your window is dirty.

filter. At some point you need to look in the mirror and say, "Maybe I'm the one who needs to change. If I'm always critical, maybe I've developed a habit of seeing the negative rather than the positive. Maybe I've trained myself to be cynical and sarcastic rather than kind and loving. Maybe my filter is dirty."

It's amazing the difference that it makes when you get up every morning and put on a fresh new attitude. *I'm excited about today. I don't have to go to work, but I get to go to work. I'm grateful to have a job. I'm not going to complain about the traffic. I'm grateful to have a car. I'm not going to focus on what's wrong. Father, I want to thank You for what's right in my life.* You know what you're doing? You're cleaning your window.

The Arrangement in Your Mind

A ninety-two-year-old man was moving into a home for seniors. Although he could see images, he was legally blind. His wife of seventy years had just passed away.

After he waited patiently in the lobby, a young nurse came and took him to his room. As he maneuvered his walker through the hallways, she began to describe the details of his room. She told how it had a beautiful window and a nice couch and a desk area. Right in the middle of her description, he interrupted her and said, "I love it! I love it! I love it!" She laughed and said, "Sir, you haven't seen the room yet. Wait just a moment. We're almost there." He said, "No, whether I like my room or not doesn't depend on how the furniture is arranged. It depends on how my mind is arranged."

That's the way we should live. *I've already made up my mind to enjoy this day. I've already made up my mind to have a blessed year.* Life is too short for you to live it sour, discouraged, and letting your circumstances dictate your attitude. Every morning you have to make the decision, "This is the day the Lord has made. I'm going to live it in faith. I'm going to be positive. I'm going to see the good. I'm going to make the most of this day." That man could have been sour because he had lost his sight, bitter because his wife had passed, and discouraged because he was moving out of his house. He learned this secret: Every day he put on a fresh new attitude.

> He learned this secret: Every day he put on a fresh new attitude.

"Joel, I had a bad childhood, my spouse walked away, and I came down with an illness." We can all find reasons to have a chip on our shoulder, to live sour. You have to let things go. What happened in your past cannot change what God has in your future. God wouldn't have allowed it if it was going to keep you from your destiny. But if we go around discouraged and asking, "Why did this person do me wrong? Why did I lose a loved one? Why did my business slow down?" it will sour our attitude and keep us from the new things God has in store. The Scripture says, "Rain falls on the just and the unjust." No one is exempt from difficulties. But if you stay in faith, that setback is going to set you up for God to show out in your life. Instead of being sour, put on a new attitude: *God, You said You would give me beauty for these ashes. You said You would take what was meant for my harm and turn it to my advantage. So, Lord, I thank You that I'm not just coming out, but I'm coming out better.*

Don't Feed on What Poisons

In the Scripture, Job went through a great trial. It wasn't fair. He hadn't done anything wrong, but everything came against him. At first, he got discouraged and complained. We're all human, and it's easy to have a bad attitude. But Job turned it around. When it seemed as though he was done, when it seemed there was no reason to have hope, Job looked up to the heavens and said, "I know my Redeemer lives." He was saying, "I know that God is still on the throne. I know He's bigger than what I'm facing." Job made this decision to put on a fresh new attitude. If he had become bitter and angry, we wouldn't be talking about him. When it was all said and done, Job came out with twice what he had before the trial started.

In difficult times it's tempting to get sour and say, "I don't understand it. I was doing the right thing, being my best, and this setback came out of nowhere." You have to do as Job did and draw a line in the sand and say, "I am not going to go through life with a bad attitude. I'm not going to let what's happened to me, what didn't work out, or who did me wrong keep me from becoming who I was created to be. Father, thank You that You're fighting my battles. You being for me is more than the world being against me." That's what allows God to bring you out better. But too often we're holding on to hurts, disappointments, and things we don't understand. This poisons our attitude, takes our passion, and makes us negative and critical. You have to let it go and quit going back to it. It's over and done. Move forward.

The Scripture talks about how God created you to be an eagle and to soar. A bald eagle's primary diet is live fish, but if it finds a deer carcass, it will feed on the dead flesh and often return to it. The problem is that if that deer has lead in its body from a hunter's bullet, the eagle can become desperately sick and even die from lead poisoning. If you're going to be an eagle, if you're going to soar, you can't go back to the dead things in your life that will poison you. Too many people are feeding off what didn't work out, reliving the disappointments, the failures, the bad breaks. When they wake up in the morning, the first things they think about are the hurts, the losses, the person who did them wrong. Quit feeding off that dead food. You can't put poison in your spirit and live a faith-filled life. Let it go. That's over and done. Feed on live food. The healthi-

> *If you're going to be an eagle, if you're going to soar, you can't go back to the dead things in your life that will poison you.*

est foods you can put in your spirit are God's promises. "I am blessed and cannot be cursed. Whatever I touch will prosper and succeed. Thanks be to God who always causes me to triumph. This is going to be an abundant, bountiful, flourishing year."

What are you feeding on? Pay attention to what

you're putting in your spirit. We're called to be an eagle, but sometimes we're acting like a chicken. Do you know that a chicken will eat its own waste? A chicken will feed off what's supposed to be discarded as trash. Maybe that's why a chicken has wings but is incapable of flying high or far. It holds on to what it should release. You need to view the negative things in your past as waste. No, God doesn't waste the struggles you've survived, but you're not supposed to feed off them. You've been through it, and now it's over. You've eliminated it, so now move on. Don't go back to what you released. If you're always feeding off what's been discarded, that's going to keep you from flying long and high. Reliving old hurts and thinking about what you lost will keep you on the ground. Put on a fresh new attitude, and you'll begin to rise to new heights. God didn't give you wings to stay on the ground. He didn't say you will mount up with wings as chickens. He called you an eagle. He created you to soar. Don't let a sour attitude keep you grounded. It's time to rise to new levels, to soar to new heights.

Unclog Your Heart

My father struggled with high blood pressure for his entire life. He came from a family that had a history of heart disease. When I was a teenager, we would go watch the Houston Astros play baseball. As we walked from the parking lot to the stadium, he would have to stop several times to rest. He was out of breath. It had been this way for so long that it was normal to him. Eventually he went to the doctor, and they discovered the coronary arteries to his heart were almost completely clogged. The doctor said my father's heart was operating on only 30 percent. He had open-heart surgery, the blockages were removed, and he was like a new man. He could walk for miles.

Like my father, sometimes our heart has become clogged—not physically, but with offenses, with hurts, self-pity, and discouragement. We don't realize it, but we're only operating at half of what we should be. We wonder why we don't have energy, why our marriage is stale, why we're not passionate about our dreams, not realizing there are contaminants blocking the flow. We've allowed these poisons to clog up the blessings, joy, and creativity. The good news is that you can get back to who you were created to be. You don't require a doctor. You can make these changes. If you get rid of the bitterness, the offense, the critical spirit, and the negativity, you'll get your

> We wonder why we don't have energy, why our marriage is stale, why we're not passionate about our dreams, not realizing there are contaminants blocking the flow.

passion back. You'll get that spring in your step. You'll not only enjoy life more, but you'll see God's favor and blessings in new ways.

What could you be if your heart was totally unclogged? How high could you fly if you didn't have contaminants holding you back? It's time to find out. Get up every morning and put on a fresh new attitude. This day is a gift from God. It's filled with possibilities, with new ideas, and new friendships. I'm asking you to be like that airplane and to live nose high. Stay focused on the good, focused on the possibilities. If you do this, I believe and declare you're about to see liftoff—new doors are about to open, freshness is coming in your relationships, promotion, healing, restoration, and the fullness of your destiny.

CHAPTER FOUR

Drop It

We have all had negative things happen to us. People did us wrong, the company let us go, a clerk was rude to us. It's easy to go through life offended, in self-pity, blaming ourselves, blaming our coworkers, even blaming God. Because we're always looking back, reliving the negative, we end up carrying around all this baggage that weighs us down. One of the best things you can learn to do is drop it. Let it go. Whether it happened twenty years ago or twenty minutes ago, don't carry negative baggage from yesterday into today. You won't live a victorious life if you're always reliving what didn't work out, who hurt you, and the mistakes you made. The reason it's called the past is because it's done, it's over, it's history. Now do your part and let it go.

"Joel, my fiancé walked out on me. He broke my heart. That's why I'm bitter." They hurt you once, but don't let them continue to hurt you by always thinking about it. That's going to keep you down, discouraged, with no passion. As long as you're dwelling on it, you're going to miss the new things God wants to do. God says He will give you beauty for ashes. He says He will take what was meant for your harm and use it to your advantage. But you have to do your part and drop it. Quit thinking about it, quit reliving it, and move forward. There's a new beginning in front of you. But God will not release new opportunities as long as you're reliving old hurts and old failures.

You may have a lot of negative things in your past that weren't fair—you had a rough childhood, your business didn't make it, you lost a loved one. You could easily go through life with a chip on your shoulder, not trusting anybody, bitter, resentful. But everything you went through deposited something inside. You're not defined by your past; you're prepared by your past. You're stronger, you're more experienced, and you have greater confidence. If that hadn't happened, you wouldn't be prepared for the new levels that are coming your way. Don't go around with a "poor old me" mentality, feeling sorry for yourself. I've heard it said that you can be pitiful or you can be powerful, but you can't be both. You may have made some mistakes. Perhaps you blew your marriage and didn't raise your children right. You have a lot of regrets. You can't do anything about what happened yesterday. Living guilty and condemned is not going to make anything better. It's time to drop it. If you get rid of that negative baggage, you'll not only feel a weight lift off you, but you'll step into the new things God has in store.

Come Over into the *Is*

The Scripture says, "Where the Spirit of the Lord is, there is freedom." It doesn't say where the Spirit of the

Lord *was*. If you're always thinking about yesterday, last month, or last year, there's no freedom there. That's where the Spirit of the Lord *was*. This is a new day. There are new victories, new relationships, and new opportunities. Quit living in what was and come over into what is. Right now there is freedom for you. Right now there are new beginnings. Right now there is joy, peace, and restoration. Crying over what happened yesterday doesn't bring freedom. Living in regrets of what you should have done or what could have been isn't at all productive. Being offended, upset, and frustrated over what didn't work out will only keep you in mediocrity. It's time to drop it and move forward. You may be a product of your past, but you don't have to be a prisoner of your past. Nothing that has happened to you was a surprise to God. When He laid out the plan for your life, He already knew every person who would hurt you, every loss you would go through, and every mistake you would make. The good news is that for every

> *You may be a product of your past, but you don't have to be a prisoner of your past.*

setback, God has already arranged a comeback. For every disappointment, He has a new beginning. For every failure, He'll bring a restoration. For all the ashes, He has beauty.

You have to put your foot down and say, "That's it. I may have been through some disappointments, and I may have made some mistakes, but I'm not going to waste the time I have left worrying about what I could have done better, bitter over what didn't work out, or upset over who did me wrong. I'm leaving the *was* and I'm coming over into the *is*. I'm dropping the offense, dropping the self-pity, dropping the blame, dropping the failure. I'm done carrying negative baggage. I'm going to live my life free." Here's the key: If somebody did you wrong, leave it up to God. He'll be your vindicator. If you made mistakes, quit beating yourself and receive God's mercy. It's new every morning. If there are things you don't understand—you worked hard, but you didn't get the promotion, or you did your best, but your marriage didn't make it—instead of dragging around that negative baggage, you have to be mature enough to say, "God, I don't understand it, but I trust You. I know that You wouldn't have allowed it if it wasn't going to somehow work to my advantage. So I'm not going to get bitter, and I'm not going to live looking back in my rearview mirror. I'm going to keep moving forward, knowing that my best days are still ahead."

The writer of Ecclesiastes says, "Better is the end than the beginning." You may have had a rough start, but you don't have to have a rough finish. Better is the end. Maybe you had a disappointment: Somebody broke your heart, a dream didn't work out, or the medical report wasn't good. Don't get stuck in what happened yesterday. Don't keep dwelling on the negative. God is saying, "Something better is coming." There may be some rough spots in the middle, but don't stay focused on the betrayal—better is coming. The loan didn't go through, but don't sit around in self-pity—better is coming. You prayed and believed, but the medical report wasn't good. That's one report, but God has another report. He says that better is coming. Now don't cancel out the better by living in yesterday and dwelling on the negative—the regrets, the failures, what didn't work out. If your mind is always in yesterday, you're going to move in that direction. You can't go forward looking backward. If you're always thinking about what didn't work out, reliving how someone hurt you, or telling your friends how bad the medical report

> *Now don't cancel out the better by living in yesterday and dwelling on the negative— the regrets, the failures, what didn't work out.*

is, you're going to get stuck. Receive this into your spirit: Better is coming. Healing is coming, breakthroughs are coming, and new opportunities are coming.

Become an Expert at Dropping It

The apostle Paul says in Philippians, "I focus all my energies on this one thing, forgetting what lies behind and reaching forward to what lies ahead." Here's a man who wrote nearly half the books of the New Testament. He could have said, "I focus all my energy on being a better writer, on improving my leadership skills, and on impacting the culture more effectively." But he said instead, in effect, "What's more important than all of that is letting go of what lies behind." He knew that if we carry negative baggage, it will keep us from our destiny. Paul had been through a lot of adversity. He had been falsely accused of crimes, beaten with rods, put in prison, often gone without food, shipwrecked, on and on. If he hadn't learned this principle, he would have become bitter and discouraged, saying, "God, why is this happening to me? Look what I've been through. It's not fair."

Other translations of Paul's statement highlight just how strongly he felt: "This one thing I do: forgetting what lies behind." He was saying, "I don't do everything right yet, but this one thing I'm good at, this one thing I have down: I know how to let go of the past." Paul was an expert at dropping it. Sometimes we spend more energy holding on to the negative past than we do letting it go. What if we would do as Paul did and start focusing that energy on dropping the offense, dropping the guilt, dropping the self-pity, dropping the hurt, and moving forward?

How do you drop it? Quit thinking about it, and quit talking about it. Don't rehearse negative things that have happened to you. The reason some people never see the better is because they're always opening old wounds. Every week they call their friends and say, "Can you believe what they did to me?" It happened twenty-seven years ago, but they're

> *What if we would do as Paul did and start focusing that energy on dropping the offense, dropping the guilt, dropping the self-pity, dropping the hurt, and moving forward?*

still dragging it up as though it happened yesterday. If you're going to get free, you need to not only drop it— you need to bury it. Have a funeral for it. Put it away once and for all. Decide that you're not going to talk about it one more time. When you're tempted, zip it up. That betrayal, that disappointment, and that injustice is dead. It's over, it's in the past, and it's buried. If you go dig it up, it's going to stink. It's not only going to make you sour, but nobody's going to want to be around you. When you're carrying around stinky stuff, you may not realize it, but that makes you stink. When you're bitter, you push people away. When you're offended, upset, and holding a grudge, that pushes opportunities away. You have to get the stink out of your life. Leave the baggage.

Several years ago I was coming home from a Night of Hope. We usually leave home on Thursday and come back on Friday night after the event. On this trip, I had forgotten to take any extra socks. I put my socks on Thursday morning and traveled to the city, did a book signing that day, and had several other activities. The next morning I put the same socks on, went to a gym and worked out, then later I did the Night of Hope and shook hands with hundreds of people afterward. It was a hot evening, and I had perspired a lot. When we finally got on the plane to fly home, I was tired. I took off my shoes, put my feet on the chair in front of me, and Victoria nearly passed out. She exclaimed, "Joel, put your shoes back on! Your feet stink so bad!" I said, "They don't stink. They smell fine." I couldn't smell a thing. The problem is that when you stink, many times you don't know it. When you're mad at somebody, offended at your neighbor, carrying unforgiveness and bitterness, you may not realize it, but it's making your life stink. It's pushing people and opportunities away. Why don't you let go of the stinky stuff? There's an amazing future in front of you—beauty for ashes, joy for mourning, dancing for heaviness—but you have to move forward.

Maybe you need to bury that mistake you made. You've lived guilty, condemned, and down on yourself long enough. Have a funeral and put it behind you. No more talking about it. No more letting the accuser make you feel unworthy by telling you, "You don't deserve to be blessed. You're a failure." Those lies will stink up your life. Quit letting the negative play. When the defeat, the mistake, or the hurt comes back up on the movie screen of your mind, do yourself a favor and change

> *When the defeat, the mistake, or the hurt comes back up on the movie screen of your mind, do yourself a favor and change the channel.*

the channel. Have the attitude, *I'm not going backward. I'm not living in regrets. I'm not rehearsing failures. I'm moving forward. I may have had some bad breaks, but I know better is the end.* If you get your mind going forward, your life will go forward.

Pay attention to what you're dwelling on all day. Listen to what you're saying. How much time and energy are you giving to the negative things of your past—guilt, offense, blame, discouragement? You only have so much emotional energy each day. When you spend that energy on negative things, calling a friend to talk about what somebody did to you three years ago, rehearsing failures, being down on yourself, that's energy you should be using to move forward. You have to get out of the *was* and step into the *is*. Don't say another word about that breakup and disappointment you went through. Don't tell another person about the mistake you made. That's over and done. You had a funeral. You buried them. Now don't talk about them anymore. Don't relive those losses one more time in your mind.

You determine what you think about. You can't stay

focused on the negative and expect to go forward. The truth is that every person has baggage. We've all had things happen that can weigh us down and cause us to be bitter. The difference between people who are positive, happy, and expecting good things and people who are negative, discouraged, and bitter is simple. People who are negative hold on to the baggage, while positive people have learned to drop it, to let it go.

Drop It, Leave It, Let It Go

In Mark 11, Jesus was talking about what we should do when somebody does us wrong. He says, "Forgive them and let it drop. Leave it. Let it go." Notice the principle: Drop it, leave it, let it go. When somebody is talking badly about you, it's easy to get upset and be offended. Try a different approach—drop it, leave it, let it go. God will fight your battles. Someone betrayed you and walked away. Don't spend another day bitter. You're not hurting them; you're poisoning yourself. Drop it, leave it, let it go.

You took a step of faith, started a business, but it didn't work out. Don't let that sour your life. Do three simple things: Drop it, leave it, let it go. God has something better. You prayed, but your loved one didn't make it or the relationship didn't work out. You could be bitter and say, "God, why don't You answer my prayers?" Drop it, leave it, let it go.

The reason the Scripture says to "leave it" is because you're going to be tempted to pick it back up. You may drop it at first, but the next morning when you think about what they said, you'll want to pick up the hurt and the bitterness. I know people who have been picking up the same offense for forty-seven years. It's not a bag anymore; it's a part of

> *The reason the Scripture says to "leave it" is because you're going to be tempted to pick it back up.*

who they are. You have to leave it. It may not have been fair, but God saw what happened. He's a God of justice. He'll make your wrongs right. When you leave it, that doesn't mean you're weak, or that you're giving in, or that you don't care about what they did to you. No, you're saying, "God, I trust You to be my vindicator. I trust that You will open new doors and get me to where I'm supposed to be."

Imagine that at ten o'clock on a Monday morning a coworker is rude to you. Drop it, leave it, let it go. When you see your coworker again at noon, you'll be tempted to pick it back up. Just say, "No, thanks. I'm leaving that offense where I dropped it. I'm not carrying around any baggage." Later that same day, you have a disappointment, finding out that you didn't get a contract. You could be sour and let it ruin your week. Instead, you drop it, leave it, let it go. When you wake up on Tuesday morning, that disappointment will be waiting for you, reminding you, "It didn't work out. You have a right to be discouraged. Nothing good is in your future." You need to reply, "No, thanks. I'm not picking that back up. I'm leaving the discouragement right there. I know God has something better."

Think of how many people get cut off in traffic at eight in the morning and still are upset at noon. Instead of dropping it and leaving it, they picked up the offense, put it in their bag, and are carrying it around. A coworker was rude to them on Monday, and for the whole next week they're sour. They keep picking it back up. Life is too short for you to carry around that baggage. Your time is too valuable and your destiny is too important to go through the day weighed down by offenses, bitterness, guilt, and anger. This doesn't happen automatically. You have to make the decision to not only drop it but to leave it. Don't give in to the temptation to pick it back up.

Don't Get Caught Up in the Whys

There was a man in the Scripture named Ahithophel, who was one of King David's right-hand men. For over twenty-five years he served as an advisor and close counselor to David. But when David's son Absalom attempted to take over the throne, Ahithophel was one of the first to desert David and go with his son. Ahithophel began to advise Absalom on the steps he should take to overthrow his father, but when Absalom chose another advisor's counsel over his, Ahithophel was so distraught by the rejection that the Scripture says he went out and hung himself.

After so many years, why would a trusted advisor of King David suddenly turn on him? Many scholars believe that Ahithophel was the grandfather of Bathsheba, the woman whom David had an affair with and whose husband, Uriah, he had killed. Then David took her as his wife. Could it be the reason Ahithophel turned on David so easily was because he never got past what David did to Bathsheba and Uriah? Instead of forgiving David, dropping it, leaving it, letting it go, all those years that poison was simmering inside. Ahithophel smiled on the outside and gave David advice, but inside something wasn't right. He ended up tragically taking his own life.

What David did was wrong. In the natural, Ahithophel had a reason to be upset, angry, and bitter. But when you carry around that negative baggage year after year, you're not hurting the other person, you're contaminating your own life. You don't have the creativity, the favor, and the blessing you should. As with Ahithophel, what somebody did to you may have been wrong, and it may not be easy, but for your sake, not theirs, you need to drop it, leave it, let it go. When you do, God will heal your hurts. He'll restore your broken pieces. He'll pay you back for the injustice. When you hold on to unforgiveness, bitterness, and anger, you're not holding it; it's actually holding you. That poison will lead you down the wrong path. Ahithophel had everything going for him, was a successful and respected advisor to the

> *When you carry around that negative baggage year after year, you're not hurting the other person; you're contaminating your own life.*

king, but because he wouldn't let go of his negative baggage, it cost him his life. He missed his destiny. Don't let that be you. Don't play around with negative baggage—bitterness, unforgiveness, guilt. Let it go.

"But, Joel, I don't understand why all this happened to me. Why did this person do me wrong? Why did I come down with this illness?" People ask me, "Why did your mother get healed, but my mother didn't?" We're never going to understand everything. Don't get caught up in the whys of life. The Scripture says, "We see in part now, through a glass dimly, but one day we will see in full." One day it will be clear. If you're always trying to figure out the whys, you're going to get frustrated and bitter. The best thing you can do is drop it. Leave it alone. If God wants you to know why, He's God, and He'll tell you why. But if He's not revealing it to you, you need to let it go. Some things God doesn't want you to know. The writer of Proverbs says, "It is God's privilege to conceal things." If you're going to trust God, you have to accept that there are going to be unanswered questions. We have to be mature enough to say, "God, I don't understand why this happened, but I'm okay without understanding why. I don't have to have all the answers. You're God, and I'm not. I trust that Your ways are better than mine."

I know a couple who pastor a church in another city. One night their teenage son was killed in a car accident. You can imagine how devastated and heart-broken they were. Overnight, their world came crashing down. They're great people, strong believers. I didn't know how they were going to respond. Many people would get angry, blame God, and let that sour the rest of their lives. It wasn't easy for them. They went through a dark time, but they came through it. I asked them how they did it without becoming bitter. They said, "We made the decision that we weren't going to exchange what we do know for what we don't know. We do know that God is good, that He's loving, that He's merciful, and that He's for us. We're not going to let one situation that we don't understand cancel all that out." Maybe there's something you've gone through that doesn't make sense, and it's bothering you, causing you to doubt, to live discouraged. You need to do what they did. Quit trying to figure it out and go back to what you do know. God is for you. He has you in the palms of His hands. He wouldn't have allowed that if He wasn't going to somehow use it to your advantage.

Have an "I Don't Understand It" File

The fact is that everything in our life is not going to fit perfectly into our theology. We all should have a file in our thinking that's labelled our "I Don't Understand It" file. When things come up that don't make sense, and you can't find an answer, instead of trying to figure it out, getting confused and frustrated, just put it in your "I Don't Understand It" file and keep moving forward. If you make the mistake of going through life trying to figure out why something bad happened, why the relationship didn't work out, or why your loved one didn't get healed, that's going to poison your life.

> *The fact is that everything in our life is not going to fit perfectly into our theology.*

In 1881, James Garfield was elected the twentieth president of the United States. Six months later, he was shot in the back. The doctors were able to save his life, but they couldn't find the bullet that was lodged behind his pancreas. He was recovering fine, but back in those days they thought if they didn't remove the bullet, it would cause him problems. They did more surgeries, poked and probed all around, but still couldn't find it. Alexander Graham Bell created an electrical device to try to locate it, but that didn't work. Eighty days after being shot, President Garfield died, not from his original wound, but from the infection and slow blood poisoning that came from all the probing around.

Sometimes it's better to leave things alone. The problem is that if you're always probing around your wounds, your hurts, your disappointments, trying to figure out why, trying to get answers, you're keeping it stirred up, and you're never going to heal. You need to let it go. Give it to God and say, "God, I don't understand it, but I'm not going to keep probing. I'm not going to try to figure it out. I know that You wouldn't have allowed it if You couldn't bring good out of it, so I'm going to drop it, leave it, and let it go."

My challenge for you today is to quit looking back. Get out of the *was* and come over into the *is*. God wants to do something new, but you have to let go of the old. Don't be like Ahithophel and hold on to things that are going to poison your life. Be like the apostle Paul and focus your energies on letting go of what lies behind. Is there something you need to drop—a hurt, a failure, a disappointment, an offense? There's no better time than now. Today can be a turning point. You can close this chapter free. Make a decision that you're getting rid of all the negative baggage. You're going to drop it and leave it. You're not going to go back and pick it up again. You're going to let God be your vindicator, and you're going to receive His mercy for mistakes you've made. If you do this, I believe and declare God is going to heal your hurts. He's going to give you beauty for the ashes. He's going to release new relationships and new opportunities. As Ecclesiastes says, "Better is coming." Joy is coming, healing is coming, favor is coming, the fullness of your destiny is coming.

CHAPTER FIVE

The Right Recording

There is a recording constantly playing in our mind telling us who we are. The problem for some people is that their recording is negative. It's been that way for so long they don't realize it. Something is always telling them, "You're not attractive. You don't have a good personality. You've made too many mistakes. You're the wrong nationality." The recording plays over and over. They wonder why they don't feel good about themselves, and it's because of what's playing. Some of this started back in childhood. Somebody told them they weren't smart. "You'll never do much in life. You're not talented enough."

This is what happened to a friend of mine in our senior year of high school. Everyone in our class went to the counselor and discussed what we wanted to do in life. My friend told the counselor that he wanted to become a doctor. The counselor may have meant well, but he told my friend that he didn't have the skills to do that and that he should look at a field where he did physical work. My friend came back so deflated. He didn't know any better. He let that recording play in his mind over and over—*You don't have the skills. You're not good enough.* Because of those negative words, he never went after his dreams.

Are you letting what somebody said about you hold you back? Have you allowed it to become part of the recording that plays in your mind? The good news is that you control your recording. You don't have to let those thoughts keep playing. The key is to turn off the old recording and put on a new one. Here's what should be playing in your mind: *I am talented. I am valuable. I am attractive. I am blessed. I have a good personality. People like me.* Pay attention to what's playing in your mind. Don't go through life being against yourself, focused on all your faults, feeling inferior, and saying "nothing good is going to happen." Too many people feel wrong inside. There's a nagging feeling that's always reminding them of what they're not and how they don't measure up.

I say this with humility, but I like myself. I feel good about who I am. I'm proud of who God made me to be. If you don't love yourself in a healthy way, you're not going to love others. You won't have good relationships if you go around feeling guilty, unattractive, and not up to par. The reason some people don't get along with others is because they don't get along with themselves. If you don't like yourself, you're not going to like me, even though I'm nice. You have to be at peace with yourself before you can have peace with others. If you're hard on yourself, you'll be hard on others. If you feel wrong about who you are, you'll be critical and find fault with

> *If you don't love yourself in a healthy way, you're not going to love others.*

others. You owe it to yourself, and you owe it to your spouse, to your children, and to your friends, to turn off the negative recording. It's poisoning who you are. When you feel good about yourself, when you know you're valuable, attractive, talented, and one of a kind, then you can love others. When you have the right recording, you'll have healthy relationships.

Take inventory of what's playing in your mind. If you find defeating thoughts of being unworthy and not good enough, delete them. Quit dwelling on them. Then take it one step further and put on a new recording. You'll be amazed at what happens when you go through the day playing what God says about you. The psalmist says, "You have been fearfully and wonderfully made." Instead of that recording, your recording is saying, "You're ordinary. There's nothing special about you. You're not that attractive." Delete, delete, delete. Put on the new recording that says, "I am fearfully and wonderfully made. I'm a masterpiece. I'm one of a kind. I have seeds of greatness."

Believe That You Are Marvelous

In Psalm 139, David says, "God, You have made me in an amazing way. What You have done is wonderful." Other versions use the word *marvelous*. Imagine going through the day with those words playing in your mind: *I'm amazing. I'm marvelous. I'm wonderful.* Most of us are not bold enough to think that highly about ourselves. We don't have any problem thinking about our faults, what we did wrong, and how we don't measure up. But when this new recording comes, the enemy will work overtime to try to keep you from playing it. He doesn't want you to feel good about yourself. It's going to take boldness to believe that you're amazing, you're marvelous, and you're wonderfully made. I'm not saying to do it arrogantly, but if you're going to become who you were created to be, you're going to have to get in agreement with God. You can't go around intimidated, thinking you're average and don't have much to offer. I dare you to start playing the right recording: *I'm amazing. I'm marvelously made. I'm a masterpiece.*

It's very simple. The enemy wants you to feel wrong about yourself; God wants you to feel right about yourself. When He created you, He stepped back and said, "That was very good." When you wake up in the morning, instead of looking in the mirror and thinking, *Look how old I'm getting. Look at all these wrinkles. Look at how overweight I am*, why don't you look in the mirror and say, "Good morning, you amazing thing. Good morning, you fearfully and wonderfully made child of the Most High God"? You're not bragging on you; you're bragging on what God has done. When you feel good about yourself, you'll go further, you'll have better relationships, and you'll enjoy life more. It all starts inside.

> *Why don't you look in the mirror and say, "Good morning, you amazing thing. Good morning, you fearfully and wonderfully made child of the Most High God"?*

A young lady came for prayer during one of our services. She was in her twenties and strikingly beautiful, like she could be a model on the cover of a fashion magazine. I asked what she wanted prayer for. She told how she had such low self-esteem and how she felt so unattractive. She was dealing with an eating disorder and had been cutting herself. I thought to myself, *You can't find a more beautiful girl, but she let the wrong recording play, and now it's stuck in her head.* Over and over, she was hearing, "You're not attractive. You're not valuable. Nobody cares about you." They were all lies, but what plays in our mind is very powerful. A wrong recording can mess up your life. You have to be beautiful inside before you can be beautiful outside. She had all the natural beauty in the world; her problem was that she was unattractive inside. Sometimes we think that if we can get the outside fixed up, we'll feel good about ourselves, but it's just the opposite. If you get the inside fixed, if you put on the right recording, it will fix the outside.

We all spend time every morning getting dressed and ready for our day. We take a shower, shave or put makeup on, and decide which clothes to wear. We put effort into getting the outside looking the best we can, and that's good. But a pretty face can't hide low self-esteem, and wearing the latest fashions won't cover up feeling unattractive. I wonder what would happen if we took five minutes every morning to get our inner person ready for the day. What would happen if before we leave the house, we remind ourselves of who we are? "I am strong. I am talented. I am attractive. I am disciplined. I am focused. I am beautiful. I am amazing. I am fearfully and wonderfully made." Take time to make these positive affirmations over yourself. If you do it in the morning, it will get that recording started in the right direction. The more you do it, the more it will become a part of who you are. Just as the negative gets down into your subconscious and holds you back, this positive will push you forward. It's good to make a list and have it on your phone, to post it on your bathroom mirror and on your computer at work. Several times a day, read it over

> *The more you dwell on the right thoughts, the less room there is for the wrong thoughts.*

and get it down in your spirit. The more you dwell on the right thoughts, the less room there is for the wrong thoughts.

How Do You See Yourself?

Some ladies have never thought, *I'm beautiful. I'm attractive. I'm amazing.* They would say, "That's not me, Joel. I'm ordinary. There's nothing attractive about me." The problem is that wrong recording is keeping you from shining. Every person is made in the image of God. You are beautiful in your own way. You have a beautiful smile, you have a beautiful spirit, and you have beautiful skin. Everybody has something that makes them attractive. Delete the thoughts that are telling you, *You're unattractive. You're too big. You're too small.* Put on a new recording that says, *I'm beautiful. I'm attractive. I'm amazing. I'm valuable.* You've let the lies play long enough. Start playing what God says about you over and over.

Ladies, don't ever tell your husband that you're

unattractive. Don't ever put yourself down in front of him. He didn't marry you because you were unattractive. He married you because he sees your beauty. He sees what God put in you. You may not be able to see it yet. But when you tell him that you don't feel attractive and you don't think you look good, all that's doing is pushing him away. The last thing you want is for him to start agreeing with you. What if he said, "Yes, you're right. You are kind of homely"? That would start another world war. You may not feel beautiful, but you need to start acting like you're beautiful, dressing like you're beautiful, and thinking like you're beautiful. Change the recording. When you are beautiful inside, it will start showing outside. You carry yourself the way you feel about yourself. If you feel unattractive, you're sending messages out even subconsciously that say you're unattractive. If you feel inferior, intimidated, and untalented, you project that everywhere you go. It will show out in your posture, in your body language, and in your personality. People will treat you based on what you're sending out.

I met a young lady once who, and I say this

respectfully, wasn't necessarily attractive outside. She didn't have a lot of natural beauty, but on the inside she had it going on. She wasn't arrogant, but she was confident. She knew she was made in the image of God. She knew she was crowned with favor. She may have looked ordinary, but she thought extraordinary. She carried herself like a queen. She walked like she was royalty. She dressed like she was headed for the runway. She may have bought an outfit secondhand, but she wore it like it was brand-new. What made the difference? Inside she sees herself as a beautiful, talented, creative, intelligent child of the Most High God. What's inside is going to show up eventually outside. Because she has the right recording, she naturally exudes confidence, strength, beauty, and ability.

The way you see yourself is the way other people are going to see you. If you see yourself as attractive, talented, and with it, people are going to see you that way. That's what you're going to send out. Quit putting yourself

> *The way you see yourself is the way other people are going to see you.*

down. Quit letting those negative thoughts about you play. When you criticize yourself, you are criticizing God's creation. You have enough people and circumstances against you, so don't be against yourself. When the negative comes up, do yourself a favor and delete it. Switch over to the right recording.

Get Good at Hitting the Delete Button

Kobe Bryant was one of the greatest basketball players who's ever played the game. On July 1, 2014, he posted a picture on social media of him holding his Los Angeles Lakers jersey. The caption read, "On this day eighteen years ago, right after being drafted, the Charlotte Hornets basketball team told me they had no use for me and traded me." He had a pleasant smile on his face. After being told he wasn't useful, he went on to win five NBA championships with the Lakers. He was an eighteen-time NBA all-star, the league's most valuable player in 2008, a two-time scoring champion, and on and on. I wonder what would have happened if he'd let those phrases constantly play in his mind: *We have no use for you. You're not that good. You don't have what it takes.* That could have kept him from his destiny. What Kobe did was to hit the delete button. "That's not going on my hard drive. I know I'm valuable. I know I have what it takes."

Kobe understood this principle: You can't play negative, defeating, limiting words and reach your potential. Words are like seeds. They have power. If you let them take root, they'll grow and become what was said. That's great when those words are positive and push you forward. But every person has negative words spoken over them as well as people who try to hold them back and discourage them. Do as Kobe did—delete the negative and become who God created you to be.

I know a minister who, when he was young, traveled with an older, very well-known minister. He was his assistant and went with him everywhere. He

> *Words are like seeds. They have power. If you let them take root, they'll grow and become what was said.*

was in the background, but deep down he believed that one day he would have a prominent ministry. Being in the shadows of the minister who was so talented and popular, he had to fight feeling intimidated and thinking he didn't have what it takes. One night after a service, a city leader came behind the stage looking for the older minister, but he had already left. This young man greeted him and asked if he could help him. The city leader said that he wanted prayer for a situation in his family. The young minister's eyes lit up, and he said, "I'll pray for you." The man shook his head and said, "No, son, you won't do." Those words were like daggers. He already felt insecure and was already doubting whether he could do it. He let that phrase become a part of his recording. Over and over, *You won't do. You don't have what it takes.* Year after year, anytime he tried to get his confidence up and step out, that phrase, *You won't do*, would get louder and louder inside, and he would shrink back.

One day the young minister did what I'm asking you to do. He realized that people don't determine your destiny. Negative words spoken over you only have power if you give them power, if you start believing them. He hit the delete button and started a new recording: *I am anointed. I am talented. I am favored. I am exceptional. I have seeds of greatness. I am strong in the Lord.* He changed his recording. New doors started to open, and he went on to become one of the most prominent ministers of our day. Years later, the city leader who had said, "You won't do," invited him to come speak at a very prestigious event. One day some of the people who are dismissing you, not giving you credit, and trying to make you feel less-than are going to want what you have. God is preparing a table before you in the presence of your enemies.

The key is that you can't let something negative spoken over you become a part of your recording. You have to get good at hitting the delete button. It may have come from somebody who should have been speaking faith into you—a parent, a coach, a teacher, a colleague. People should have been encouraging you, but instead they told you what you can't become, what you can't do, how you don't measure up. Quit dwelling on it. Quit replaying it. They don't know what God put in you. Sometimes people say negative things because they don't feel good about themselves. They have their own issues—they're insecure, they're hurting, they've got a wrong recording, and they're just passing it on. Don't take it personal. Hit the delete button and keep playing what God says about you. They say, "You don't have what it takes." Delete. You say, "I am fully loaded and totally equipped." "You're average. Nothing special about you." Delete. "I'm exceptional. I'm a masterpiece." "We don't have any use for you. You won't do." Delete. "I am talented. I have seeds of greatness."

Shut the Door to Negativity

Are you allowing what people have said or the way they've treated you to cause you to not believe in yourself and not pursue your dreams? Turn off that recording. The enemy wouldn't be trying to stop you if he didn't know there was something amazing in your future. He'll use people, negative words, and how you were treated, left out, and discounted to try to get that negative recording playing. He knows there is nothing more powerful than what you believe about yourself. What you're dwelling on all day is determining whether or not you'll become who you were created to be. Don't let what someone said cause you to feel less-than. That's held you back long enough. It's time to put on a new recording. You are equipped, you are empowered, you are anointed, you have what it takes, and you've been crowned with favor. God is breathing in your direction. He calls you a masterpiece. If anyone calls you something different, delete it. If they

> *He knows there is nothing more powerful than what you believe about yourself.*

make you feel any different, delete it. You need to protect your recording. Don't let it become contaminated.

Nobody can make you think something. Other people can't make you feel inferior, make you feel not valuable, or make you feel untalented; you have to give them permission. Quit permitting what you should be deleting. You don't let everyone in your house. If a

stranger showed up at your door holding poison, a rattle-
snake, or a stick of dynamite, you wouldn't say, "Come
on in. You're welcome to my house." You would shut the
door, lock it, and make sure they couldn't get in. What
are you letting into your mind? Are you welcoming poison, the negative things people have said? Are you letting
into your home the lies that say you're not talented, you
won't do, you're the wrong nationality? Why don't you
start shutting the door and saying "No thanks"? The
Scripture says to guard your mind. You have to be selective about what you allow in.

A few years ago we kept a couple of rabbits in a
fenced-in area of our backyard. I noticed one of them
looked as though he wasn't feeling well. He kept rubbing
the side of his face as though something was bothering
him, so we took him to the veterinarian. The vet gave
him some antibiotics and said he should get better. We
tried that for a week, but it didn't help. Then the rabbit's
face began to swell up so much that he had a big growth
on top of his nose. We took him back, and the vet exam-
ined him further. He found that an egg from a fly had

somehow gotten up in the rabbit's nasal passage, and that a larva was growing and about to hatch. Once they got to the root of the problem, they removed it, and the rabbit was fine.

That's the way the enemy works. He tries to plant lies in our mind that infect our thinking. *You're not good enough. You're not attractive. You'll never meet the right person. You'll never get well.* We can try to fix the outside, but until we get to the root of the problem, until we get the infection out, until we delete that recording, the lies are going to continue to limit us. Pay attention to what you're dwelling on. Ask yourself why you won't pursue your dream, why you don't feel good about yourself, or why you go around feeling guilty. If you trace it back to its beginning, you'll find a stronghold in your mind. Something has convinced you that you've made too many mistakes, and God is not going to bless you. Someone said you don't come from the right family, so you can't do anything great. That person who walked out of the relationship told you that you aren't worth loving. Those are lies that you've allowed in your mind.

The good news is that you can get rid of them. You don't have to spend another minute being infected by wrong thinking. I have the exact prescription, and it doesn't cost anything. If you start renewing your mind with what God says about you, it will clear up all the places that are infected, and it will heal all the places that are hurting. Instead of dwelling on how people said you're not valuable and how they made you feel inferior, you start to dwell on what God says about you. *I am fearfully and wonderfully made. I am a masterpiece.* That's when the infection starts to go away. Instead of letting that recording play, *You won't do. You don't have what it takes*, you play, *I'm talented. I'm creative. I'm one of a kind.* These thoughts bring healing. Whatever is holding you back, you have the prescription. Delete the lies and start taking your medicine. Dwell on what God says about you. You weren't made to go around infected. You were created to be secure, confident, talented, healthy,

> You don't have to spend another minute being infected by wrong thinking.

happy, and successful. Rise up and become who God made you to be.

No More Grasshopper Mentality

In Chapter Two, I introduced the story of how when Moses sent twelve men to spy out the Promised Land, ten came back with a negative report. They said, "We are not strong enough to take the land. All the people whom we saw are men of stature. There we saw the giants, and we were in our own sights as grasshoppers, and so we were in their sights." Notice how those spies saw themselves. They didn't say, "The giants were so big, and they called us grasshoppers. They insulted us." They said, "We were in our own sights as grasshoppers." They went into the land with a grasshopper mentality. Their thinking was contaminated before they got there. The opposition doesn't determine who you are; it simply reveals who you are. They

> *The problem is not the giants; the problem is your thinking.*

saw *all* their enemies as giants. If you have a grasshopper mentality, you're not going to see your enemies properly. They're all going to look too big. "I can't beat this cancer. Did you see the report? I can't get out of debt. I'll never accomplish this dream." The problem is not the giants; the problem is your thinking. You've been infected with grasshopper disease.

The two other spies, Joshua and Caleb, had a completely different report. They saw the same giants, yet they said, "Do not fear the people, for they are bread for us. Let us take the land." What was the difference between them and the other ten spies? Their thinking wasn't infected. They had the right recording playing. They knew the forces for them were greater than the forces against them. When you're not infected, you have a boldness, a confidence to take ground that others think is impossible. You'll be saying, "We are well able. This conflict is going to nourish us. We're going to come out stronger."

Are you in the group with Joshua and Caleb, or have you let your thinking become infected like the ten spies?

Are you playing the wrong recording? You can change. It's not hard. Start deleting the lies and replace them with what God says about you. Every morning, take time to get your inner person ready. Start the day off making positive affirmations over yourself, then all through the day keep that recording playing. Don't let the negative in. Let me help you get started with these affirmations: "I am blessed. I am prosperous. I am talented. I am creative. I am forgiven. I am redeemed. I am free. I am valuable. I am anointed. I am equipped. I am beautiful. I am attractive. I am amazing. I am fearfully and wonderfully made. I am a child of the Most High God. I have seeds of greatness. I will become all that He has created me to be."

CHAPTER SIX

The Power of the Soil

You can have a good seed that's healthy and strong, full of potential, but if it's not planted in good soil, the seed is not going to grow into what it was created to be. The problem is not with the seed. If a scientist studied the seed and ran tests, they would find that the seed is full of life. If it's an apple tree seed, it has apples in it; if it's a rose bush seed, it has blossoms in it. But if it's planted in soil that's full of rocks and thorns and weeds, it may grow a bit, but it's not going to thrive and produce what it should. It may survive, but it's not going to be healthy. It's the same principle in life. You are a seed. You are full of gifts, talents, and potential. But if you plant yourself in unhealthy soil, if you hang around friends who compromise and pull you down, if you're in an environment with limited mind-sets, surrounded by people who tell you what you can't do and how you'll never accomplish your dreams, then you won't see the growth that you should. It's not because there's something wrong with your seed—you're made in the image of God. The problem is with the soil. The thorns, the weeds, and the rocks are choking the life out of your seed.

Jesus told a parable about a man who sowed seed on good ground, and it flourished, producing a great crop. But some of the seed fell on rocky ground, and it didn't produce much. Other seed fell among the weeds and thorns, which kept the seed from growing. All the seed was the same quality; what made the difference was the soil. The thorns represent things such as friends who keep causing you to compromise, and the weeds are the coworkers who sit around and gossip and talk about how bad life is. The rocks are the relatives who tell you why you'll never break that addiction and how you'll never be successful. If you hang around negative people, they're choking out your seed. Those friends you're tempted to party with may be fun and popular, but what you can't see is that they're weeds. They're keeping you from flourishing. The environment into which you put yourself is extremely important. No matter how good a seed is, its growth is dependent on having good soil. You need to be selective with whom you give your time, energy, and attention.

> *No matter how good a seed is, its growth is dependent on having good soil.*

People are contagious. You're going to catch what they have. If your friends are prejudiced, you're going to become prejudiced. If they compromise, you're going to compromise. If they have limited mind-sets, no goals, and no motivation, their narrow-minded thinking is going to rub off on you. You're going to become like the people with whom you continually associate. Don't hang around people who don't have anything you want. If they're not making you better, if they're not inspiring you and causing you to grow, you need to make changes. You need to pull up some weeds. Get rid of those thorny friends. Quit hanging out with people who bring out the worst in you and cause you to compromise. Stay away from people who make you discouraged and try to talk you out of your dreams. Their negativity is contaminating your soil. Your destiny is too great to waste it with people who are not adding value to your life. "But, Joel, what if I hurt their feelings?" What if you miss your destiny? What if they choke out your seed? What if they keep you from blossoming?

I've heard it said that it's not enough to just focus on self-development; you have to focus on soil development. You must focus on what's around you, what's influencing you, who's speaking into your life, and to whom you're giving your time and attention. Are you putting your seed in good soil, or is it being contaminated by what you're watching, by what you're thinking about, by who you're spending time with? What you're not willing to walk away from is where you'll stop growing. If you know a friend is pulling you down, causing you to compromise, but you won't make a change, you will be stuck where you are. A seed can't grow in bad soil. If you don't empty your life of the wrong people, you'll never meet the right people. God never asks you to give up something without giving you more in return. You may go through a season of being lonely, but God will bring new friends, better friends. He'll bring you people who push you up and not pull you down, who challenge you to rise higher and not to settle for mediocrity.

Pull Up the Weeds

In the Scripture, God told Abraham to leave his country and his relatives and go to a new land. Abraham left, but as he headed out, he took along his nephew Lot. He was supposed to go with just his immediate family. It wasn't long before his workers and Lot's men had a disagreement. There was strife and arguing between their shepherds, a big conflict. Then Lot moved to a different place and got in trouble. Abraham felt responsible and had to go rescue Lot, spending all his time and energy involved in problems that he wouldn't have faced if he had left Lot behind as he was supposed to do in the first place.

Some of the difficulties we face are because we haven't been willing to leave who or what God told us to leave. Perhaps it's a friend who's not good for you. Maybe years ago, you knew you were supposed to make a change, but you kept putting it off. Now, as with Abraham, you're dealing with trouble and heartache that was unnecessary. What's interesting is the name *Lot* means "veil or covering." When you leave Lot, when you leave what you're supposed to leave, the veil will come off. You'll see things that you've never

> *Some of the difficulties we face are because we haven't been willing to leave who or what God told us to leave.*

seen—new friends, new opportunities, new talents, new levels. Are you holding on to something God is asking you to let go of? Perhaps there's someone or something that's pulling you down, keeping you from your best.

Your seed can't flourish in that soil. That's limiting your growth.

When I say leave, you don't have to make a big announcement and say, "Hey, you're contaminating me. I'm done with you. Joel told me to say good-bye to you." Leave my name out. Just slowly start spending less and less time with them. If you are stuck in a patch of weeds, it's going to choke out your dreams, your vision, and your character. It's time to pull up those weeds. That person with whom you eat lunch at the office who's always complaining about the boss, jealous of the coworkers, and mad at their spouse, I say this respectfully, but they're a weed. They're polluting your soil. They're causing you to shrivel up and fail to flourish. Yes, they are made in the image of God and can change, but until they do, you shouldn't let them contaminate you.

I'm nice to everyone, but I don't spend my time with everyone. I'm selective about whom I allow in my life. I don't spend time with negative, critical, jealous, small-minded, can't-do-it, bitter people. I value what God has given me too much to put my seed in bad soil. We have that responsibility. God has given you a gift. He could have created someone else to be alive on this day and at this time, but He chose you. Your seed is full of potential, and your seed has greatness in it. Your seed can set a new standard for your family, and your seed can break generational curses. Your seed could have the cure for cancer, and your seed could impact this world. What God has entrusted you with is extremely valuable. Do your part and keep your seed in good soil.

> *What God has entrusted you with is extremely valuable.*

Is Your Soil Contaminated?

We have a row of green bushes around our house. They've been there for years, just as healthy and lush as can be. But one day we noticed a section of the bushes started to look as though something was wrong. Those bushes were not as green and looked a little shriveled. A few weeks later, they were all dead. It was about fifteen feet of bushes out of a long row, but the plants on both sides of the dead section were fine. The landscaper came out and the first thing he said was, "I need to test the soil." He found that the soil had been contaminated in that section. We had to take the bad soil out, put in new soil, and now the plants are healthy and flourishing like all the others.

Sometimes we're wondering why we're not seeing growth, why we're not seeing favor. "God, why aren't You working?" Check your soil. Has it become contaminated? With whom are you spending your time? What are you giving your attention to? You can't watch the news all the time and expect to live a positive, faith-filled life. After about twenty minutes, you're going to be depressed. Pay attention to your environment. The seed can't grow in that negative soil. What are you taking in all day?

A man told me that for twenty years he listened to talk radio for an hour each way during his daily commute. It was a political station where people were arguing about politics and often being disrespectful to one another. This man would get so wrought up and angry. By the time he got to work, he was sour, and nobody wanted to be around him. He said, "I turned into a bitter, angry man. I didn't even like myself." One day he was flipping through the channels and accidentally came across our SiriusXM station. He had started listening over a year ago and couldn't stop. He said, "Now I'm a different person. I'm happy and friendly. People even ask me, 'What happened to you?'" What was the problem all those years? His soil. All that negativity going in was choking out his seed. It was choking his joy, his faith, and his victory.

We have enough negative things in life that we can't do anything about. If you work in an environment that's not healthy, God will give you grace for that. But I'm asking you to make good decisions about the areas of your life that you can do something about. When you're driving to work, put on something uplifting—music that inspires you or a message that builds your faith. Keep your seed in a good environment. At home, don't leave the TV on all day with the chatter, the noise, and the junk playing in the background. That's your soil. Your seed can't flourish in bad soil. This is the reason some people are not seeing God's favor. They're talented and have potential, but their soil is contaminated. Make an adjustment. God has done His part. He's given you what you need to live a victorious life. Now you need to protect that seed.

I know a professional football player who was diagnosed with cancer. He had only been in the league a few years. His dream had come true, then he was hit with this diagnosis. He could have fallen apart and gotten discouraged, but he didn't go there. He was living at home, and he told his mother that he didn't want anyone to use the word *cancer* in his house. He didn't want that word down in his spirit. He knew that if he was in a depressed atmosphere, a feel-sorry-for-me, "I'm not going to make it" environment, he wouldn't get well. His attitude was, *I am healed. I am whole. I will play football again. I will fulfill my destiny. God is bigger than what I'm facing.* What was he doing? Keeping his seed in good soil. He was creating an environment of victory. Two years later, he was back in the league.

When you face difficulties, more than ever you need

to keep your mind filled with thoughts of faith, to surround yourself with people who will speak life and hope, people who will agree with what you're believing for. You can't afford to have people who are negative, discouraging, telling you how it doesn't look good and "My grandmother died of the same thing." Do yourself a favor and stay away from them. Don't let them pollute your soil. They may be family, but you'll have to love them from a distance.

> *When you face difficulties, more than ever you need to keep your mind filled with thoughts of faith, to surround yourself with people who will speak life and hope, people who will agree with what you're believing for.*

Find the Right People

In the Scripture, Jesus went to pray for a little girl who had died. When he arrived at the house, everyone in the crowd that had gathered there was crying and upset. He told them that she wasn't dead, that she was just asleep. They began to laugh and scoff. Jesus asked them to leave the room. He only allowed the parents and Peter, James, and John to stay. He spoke to the little girl, and she was healed. Why did Jesus have the others leave? He could have healed the girl in front of everyone. He's God. It was because He was showing us the importance of having the right environment. Some people will talk you out of your dreams if you allow it. Their doubt and negativity can rub off on you. You have to set some boundaries. "I love you, but I'm not going to hang out with you. I'm not going to let you poison me. I have a destiny to fulfill. I'm going to keep my seed in good soil."

In previous chapters we saw how ten of the spies whom Moses sent to spy out the Promised Land came back with their grasshopper mentality and said there was no chance they could take the land. Even though God had promised them the victory, and even though the other two spies, Joshua and Caleb, declared they were well able to take the land, their negative report spread throughout the camp. Before long all two million people were discouraged, complaining and saying, "Moses, let's go back to Egypt and be slaves again." They never did make it into the Promised Land. What happened? Their soil became contaminated. That negative environment kept the seed from flourishing. The people with whom you surround yourself are extremely important. Don't hang around can't-do-it, not-going-to-happen, "that dream is too big for you" people. They say, "Yes, God promised it to you, but do you see how big the opposition is? You think you can get well, you can get out of debt, and you can break that addiction. I don't see how." Do yourself

> *Find people who will fan your flame, not people who will throw water on your flame.*

a favor and find some different people. Find Joshua. Find Caleb. Find people who will fan your flame, not people who will throw water on your flame. Find people who will put their faith with yours and say, "If you believe, count me in. I'm believing with you."

When Henry Ford had a dream to build a car with an engine, he started developing it, but everyone told him that it wouldn't work, that it wasn't a good idea, that nobody would want a car with a loud motor in it. He was about to stop when he attended a dinner where Thomas Edison was present. The two men had never met. Ford was introduced as the man trying to build a car that ran on gasoline. Edison peppered Ford with questions, and when Ford outlined his plan, Edison's eyes lit up. He hit his fist on the desk and said, "You've got it! A car that has its own power plant. That's a brilliant idea." Ford told how that friendship kept him going. Many of us wouldn't be driving a Ford if he hadn't found that good soil. The critics and the naysayers are a dime a dozen. Out of the twelve spies sent into the Promised Land, ten were negative. That's about average. Eighty percent will tell you what you can't do. You have to find the twenty percent who will tell you what you *can* do. Most of the time, the majority won't encourage you, because they won't see what you see. You need to find the minority who will.

Your Soil Is as Important as Your Seed

I believe one reason I've seen God's favor is because I've been in good soil. Much of it, I can't take credit for. It wasn't anything I did; it was simply the goodness of God. I was raised by parents who always told me what I could become. In a positive, loving environment, I saw my father believe for big things and break down the barriers that he was raised in. He came out of poverty and lived with an "all things are possible" mentality. Years before my father passed away, Victoria would tell me that one day I was going to pastor the church. That seemed so far out to me. I used to think, *What is she talking about? I can't get up in front of people.* But year after year, she kept telling me what I could become. When my father went to be with the Lord, I was able to step up and pastor the church. Why? My seed had been in good soil.

My sister Lisa worked at the church for seventeen years, behind the scenes with me. She was the head of volunteers and would assist my father during the services, making sure he knew everything that was going on. The Sunday after my father died, I was sitting in my father's seat in the sanctuary, about to go up and minister. Lisa was sitting right behind me, where she always sat. She said that God spoke to her heart and said, "Just as you've served your father, you are to serve your brother." For these past twenty years, Lisa has done just that— helping me, encouraging me. She could have been jealous and said, "God, I wanted to be promoted. I don't want to serve him. I want him to serve me." But instead she celebrated me. What am I saying? I didn't get where I am today by myself. I got here because I had good soil all around me. I've had people who believed in me, people who inspired me, and people who challenged me. Your soil is just as important as your seed.

Now you may have had just the opposite—people who didn't support you. Instead of telling you what you could become, they told you what you couldn't do, why you weren't going to be successful. You didn't have any choice about how you were raised. The good news is your past doesn't have to stop you. Your seed is still

alive. If you will put yourself in different soil, with
can-do people, with possi-
bility thinkers, with friends
who challenge and inspire,
with people who push you
up, then your seed will take
root and begin to blossom.
You can still see the fullness
of your destiny.

> *If you will put yourself in different soil, with can-do people, with possibility thinkers, with friends who challenge and inspire, with people who push you up, then your seed will take root and begin to blossom.*

Don't Stay in a Little Pond

This is what happened in the Scripture with Elisha. He was a farmer who was out working in the fields. It was a good place to be, but his future was limited to his family and the land he would inherit. One day the prophet Elijah came by and called out to him. Elisha saw something in Elijah that he wanted, something more than his life on the farm could provide. He saw the favor on

Elijah's life and how he was doing great things, and he connected with Elijah. He said to himself, "This is good soil. This is where I need to keep my seed." He understood the importance of his environment, the importance of the people he spent time with. For years he served the prophet Elijah. He took him food, waited on him, and wouldn't leave him. In fact, just before Elijah was taken up to Heaven, three times he told Elisha to go do his own thing, but he wouldn't do it. When Elijah went to Heaven, Elisha received a double portion of his anointing and went on to do twice as many miracles as Elijah. If Elisha had stayed in the fields, in that limited background with his family and the people he grew up with, he would never have seen the double. He had to get his seed in the right soil.

You need people in your life who are further along than you. You need people who have a bigger vision, who are more experienced, who have more wisdom, who are more mature, people whose example you can follow. You need to be exposed to new levels, so you can go to new levels. If you're the smartest one in your group, your group is too small. If you're the most successful one, you need a bigger circle. Some people want to be a big fish, not realizing they're in a little pond. Get out of that small-minded thinking. Don't be intimidated by someone who's further along; be inspired by them. You need good mentors. Get around dreamers. Connect with people who are wiser, more talented, more successful, and more experienced, then glean from them. That's good soil.

A friend of mine feeds a million children a day. He supports charities that help underprivileged children. His goal is to feed ten million a day. When I get around him, I'm inspired. It makes me dream bigger. I think, *God, You did it for him, and You can do it for me.* What is that? It's my seed getting in good soil. Does your vision increase around your friends or does it decrease? Do you leave motivated, inspired, and challenged, or are you discouraged, negative, and drained? I'm not saying every friend will inspire you, but you should have one or two who light a fire inside and push you forward. If you

> *Does your vision increase around your friends or does it decrease?*

only invest in people who are at the same level as you, you'll get stuck. Find a mentor who's been where you want to go. Just as the wrong people will pull you down, the right people will pull you up.

Peter Is Waiting for You

In Acts 3, a man who had been crippled from birth was lying by the temple gate begging for money. The apostle Peter came by and said, "I don't have any money for you, but in the name of Jesus rise and walk." Nothing happened. The man just looked at Peter, thinking, *What do you mean, rise and walk? I'm crippled. I can't walk.* That could have been the end of the story. Peter could have thought, *I did my part, but it didn't work.* But the Scripture says, "Peter took him by the right hand and lifted him up. And as he did, the man's feet and ankle bones healed." I love it that Peter wouldn't let the man stay down. He didn't give him a choice. He prayed, and then he pulled him up.

You need some friends like Peter who won't let you stay down. When you're in the pits, when you can't get up on your own, you don't need people who will feel sorry for you and get in the pits with you. You don't need people who will comfort you in the pits and tell sad stories together. You need people like Peter, who will pull you out of that pit. You need people who love you so much they won't let you make excuses. They won't let you stay discouraged, or stay addicted, or let you give up on your dream. They not only pray for you but also pull you up.

I believe that's why so many people come to our services at Lakewood and why so many watch and listen to our broadcasts, because they know we're always going to pull you up. You may be down, but we're not going to let you stay down. We're going to tell you, "Get up! There are new levels. You've been hurt. Get up. God has beauty for ashes. You had a disappointment. Get up. God has a new beginning. You've lost something. Get up. God is about to restore it. You're discouraged because you're still single. Get up. God is about to bring the right person. You're struggling in your finances. Get up. God is about to open the windows of Heaven." You need people who will help pull you into your destiny. As with this crippled man, sometimes you can't reach the next level without someone pulling you up. If you're crippled in some area, and you surround your-

> *You need people who will help pull you into your destiny.*

self with other people like you, there's no one to help you get up. You have to get around somebody stronger, somebody more successful, somebody free, so they can lift you. Lame people can't help lame people up, addicted people can't help addicted people, and depressed people can't pull depressed people up.

I'm asking you to change who you're hanging around. God has some Peters waiting for you. There are people whom He's ordained to pull you up, to lift you, and help you get on your feet. Don't sit around in your dysfunction with other dysfunctional people for the rest of your life. Your seed can't grow in that soil. Peter is out there. The right person is in place. Now you make the first move. Get out of a negative environment, get away from people who are enabling your dysfunction, get away from people who tell you that where you are is where you'll always be. Don't believe those lies. Your seed is still alive. When it hits that good soil, as with the crippled man, you're going to see things happen that you never dreamed of. You're not going to live addicted, for freedom is coming. You're not going to struggle in your health, for wholeness is coming. That lack and not having enough is not your destiny. In the good soil, you're going to see abundance, overflow, and more than enough.

Now do your part and pull up the weeds. Get rid of the thorny friends, the people who are holding you back. Empty out the negative that is weighing you down and taking up the space you need for the good things that should be in your life. Be selective about what you take in all day and stay in an environment of faith. If you do this, I declare you're about to blossom. You're going to see increase, new levels of influence, new relationships, new talents, and more joy. It's heading your way!

ACKNOWLEDGMENTS

In this book I offer many stories shared with me by friends, members of our congregation, and people I've met around the world. I appreciate and acknowledge their contributions and support. Some of those mentioned in the book are people I have not met personally, and in a few cases, we've changed the names to protect the privacy of individuals. I give honor to all those to whom honor is due. As the son of a church leader and a pastor myself, I've listened to countless sermons and presentations, so in some cases I can't remember the exact source of a story.

I am indebted to the amazing staff of Lakewood Church, the wonderful members of Lakewood who share their stories with me, and those around the world who generously support our ministry and make it possible to bring hope to a world in need. I am grateful to all those who follow our services on television, the Internet, SiriusXM, and through the podcasts. You are all part of our Lakewood family.

I offer special thanks also to all the pastors across the country who are members of our Champions Network.

Once again, I am grateful for a wonderful team of professionals who helped me put this book together for you. Leading them is my FaithWords/Hachette publisher Daisy Hutton, along with team members Patsy Jones, Billy Clark, Dale Wilstermann, and Karin Mathis. I truly appreciate the editorial contributions of wordsmith Lance Wubbels.

I am grateful also to my literary agents Jan Miller Rich and Shannon Marven at Dupree Miller & Associates.

And last but not least, thanks to my wife, Victoria, and our children, Jonathan and Alexandra, who are my sources of daily inspiration, as well as our closest family members, who serve as day-to-day leaders of our ministry, including my mother, Dodie; my brother, Paul, and his wife, Jennifer; my sister, Lisa, and her husband, Kevin; and my brother-in-law Don and his wife, Jackelyn.

We Want to Hear from You!

Each week, I close our international television broadcast by giving the audience an opportunity to make Jesus the Lord of their lives. I'd like to extend that same opportunity to you. Are you at peace with God? A void exists in every person's heart that only God can fill. I'm not talking about joining a church or finding religion. I'm talking about finding life and peace and happiness. Would you pray with me today? Just say, "Lord Jesus, I repent of my sins. I ask You to come into my heart. I make You my Lord and Savior."

Friend, if you prayed that simple prayer, I believe you have been "born again." I encourage you to attend a good Bible-based church and keep God in first place in your life. For free information on how you can grow stronger in your spiritual life, please feel free to contact us.

Victoria and I love you, and we'll be praying for you. We're believing for God's best for you, that you will see your dreams come to pass. We'd love to hear from you!

To contact us, write to:

Joel and Victoria Osteen
P.O. Box 4271
Houston, TX 77210

Or you can reach us online at www.joelosteen.com.